Nikola[...]
Three [...]

The Government I[...]
The Ga[...]

D0744718

'Two and two make five, if not the square root of five, and it all happens quite naturally in Gogol's world ... Gogol was a strange creature, but genius is always strange.' Vladimir Nabokov

'To this day people don't realise that there is no word in the dictionary to describe Gogol; we have no means of assessing all the possibilities he has exhausted; we still don't know what Gogol is, but even though we can't see him truthfully, nevertheless Gogol, albeit constricted by our poverty-stricken imagination, is closer to us than any other Russian writer.' Andrei Bely, 1910

Widely held to have led the realist revolution in Russian drama, Gogol liberated comedy from a tradition of didacticism and sentimentality. This collection, translated and introduced by Stephen Mulrine, contains Gogol's three completed plays: *The Government Inspector*, his masterpiece, satirising a corrupt society, was regarded by Nabokov as the greatest play in the Russian language; *Marriage*, 'a thoroughly improbable event in two acts', teasingly overhauls the convention of lovers united; and *The Gamblers* is a sardonic tale of the biter bit. On one level they are straightforwardly funny, peopled with witless victims of circumstance and their own folly; on another level, however, they draw us into an absurd, grotesque universe, the product of a richly surreal imagination.

Nikolai Gogol was born in Sorochintsy in the Ukraine in 1809. After a brief spell in government service in St Petersburg, he won fame as a short story writer, and in 1836, his satirical comedy *The Government Inspector* created such a furore that Gogol left Russia to settle in Rome, in self-imposed exile. *Marriage*, revised from an earlier draft titled *The Suitors*, was first performed in 1842, and *The Gamblers*, Gogol's only other completed play, was premièred in 1843. Gogol published the first part of his great picaresque novel *Dead Souls* in 1842, but religious mania in his latter years caused him to destroy its sequel and contributed to his early death in Moscow in 1852.

NIKOLAI GOGOL

Three Plays

The Government Inspector
Marriage
The Gamblers

Translated and introduced by Stephen Mulrine

Methuen Drama

METHUEN WORLD CLASSICS

1 3 5 7 9 10 8 6 4 2

This collection first published in the United Kingdom in 1999 by
Methuen Publishing Limited
215 Vauxhall Bridge Road, London SW1V 1EJ

Peribo Pty Ltd, 58 Beaumont Road, Mount Kuring-Gai,
NSW 2080, Australia, ACN 002 273 761
(for Australia and New Zealand)

The Government Inspector first published in this translation in 1997
by Nick Hern Books Limited
Translation copyright © 1997 by Stephen Mulrine
Marriage first published in this translation in this edition
Translation copyright © 1999 by Stephen Mulrine
The Gamblers first published in this translation in this edition
Translation copyright © 1999 by Stephen Mulrine

Introduction and collection copyright © 1999 by Stephen Mulrine

The right of the translator to be identified as the translator of these works
has been asserted by him in accordance with the Copyright, Designs and
Patents Act, 1988

Methuen Publishing Limited Reg. No. 3543167

A CIP catalogue record for this book
is available from the British Library

ISBN 0 413 73340 8

Typeset by Deltatype Ltd, Birkenhead, Merseyside
Printed and bound in Great Britain by
Cox & Wyman Ltd, Reading, Berks

Caution

Contents

Nikolai Gogol
Chronology

1809   20 March*: born in small market town of
Greater Sorochintsy, in Mirgorod province in
Ukraine. Father minor landowner and amateur
playwright.

1821   Enters local high school at Nezhin, gains
reputation as talented comic actor.

1828   Completes education at Nezhin, enters Petrine
Table of Ranks at fourteenth grade (equivalent
to army cornet or ensign). December: moves to
St Petersburg.

1829   June: publishes *Hans Küchelgarten*, sentimental
idyll in verse, under pseudonym. Poem attracts
hostile criticism, Gogol retrieves unsold copies
and burns them. July: leaves for Germany.
Returns to St Petersburg in September, tries
unsuccessfully to become a professional actor,
obtains clerical post in the civil service.

1831   January: appointed to teach history at the
Patriotic Institute, a young ladies' college. In
May, makes the acquaintance of Pushkin.
September: publishes first volume of *Evenings on
a Farm near Dikanka*, tales of Ukrainian village
life, widely acclaimed.

1832   March: publishes second volume.

1833   Begins writing *The Suitors*.

1834   July: through influence of literary friends,
including Pushkin and Zhukovsky, Gogol
appointed assistant professor of World History
at St Petersburg University. Future novelist and
playwright Turgenev among his first students,
but after brilliant inaugural lecture, Gogol's
shortcomings soon become evident.

1835   January: publishes *Arabesques*, including *The
Portrait*, *Nevsky Prospect* and *Diary of a Madman*.

March: publishes *Mirgorod*, two volumes, including *Taras Bulba* and *The Quarrel of the Two Ivans*. Completes revision of *The Suitors*, now titled *Marriage*. September: begins writing *The Government Inspector*, partly based on anecdote supplied by Pushkin. December: quits teaching, begins work on *Dead Souls*, also on theme suggested by Pushkin, and completes *The Government Inspector*.

1836   19 April: first performance of *The Government Inspector*, at Alexandrinsky Theatre, St Petersburg. 25 May: first performance at Maly Theatre, Moscow. The play an instant success, but Gogol deeply disturbed by reactions to it, from both ends of the political spectrum. 6 June: leaves Russia, to tour Europe. October: *The Nose* published in Pushkin's journal *The Contemporary*.

1837   26 March: settles in Rome, his permanent residence, apart from a few brief excursions, for the next eleven years.

1842   Prepares Collected Works, publishes first two volumes. May: publishes Part I of *Dead Souls*. 9 December: première of *Marriage*, in St Petersburg.

1843   January: completes publication of Collected Works, in four volumes, including *The Overcoat*, hitherto unpublished. February: *Marriage* and *The Gamblers* premièred in Moscow.

1845   July: destroys manuscript of *Dead Souls*, Part II.

1847   January: publishes *Selected Passages from Correspondence with Friends*. Comes under influence of archpriest Father Matvei Konstantinovsky, spiritual adviser. Writes apologia for his past work, published posthumously as *An Author's Confession*.

1848   January: Gogol sets out on pilgrimage to Jerusalem, fails to find spiritual consolation.

May: returns to Russia. Continues work on new version of *Dead Souls*, Part II, intended as 'Purgatorio' to 'Inferno' of Part I. Increasing religious mania and chronic illness, aggravated by fasting and ascetic practices.

1852   At his death, Gogol is said to have been so emaciated that vertebrae could be felt through his abdomen. 11 February: destroys revised version of *Dead Souls*, Part II. 21 February: dies in Moscow.

---

* Dates given 'Old Style', i.e., according to Julian calendar, used in Russia until 1918, eleven days behind modern Gregorian.

Introduction

The Russian dramatic tradition which Gogol inherited, and which he did so much to change, was itself relatively young, and the first professional theatre was established in St Petersburg only in 1756. Some fifty years earlier, as part of his drive to modernise the country, Peter the Great had built a wooden theatre in Moscow, for touring companies to perform mainly French classics, to a literally captive audience, but a genuine indigenous drama, albeit indebted to French exemplars, did not emerge until late in the eighteenth century. It did so with distinction, however, notably in the work of Denis Fonvizin, whose satirical comedy *The Brigadier* (1769) ridicules the 'Gallomania' of the day, with educated Russians aping French manners. And Fonvizin's *The Minor* (1781), arguably the best Russian comedy of the period, has been described as a critical realist work ahead of its time, attacking as it does the abuses of serf ownership and an incompetent justiciary. Similar themes engaged the attention of Vasily Kapnist, a fellow-Ukrainian and friend of Gogol's father, in his highly-regarded work *Slander* (1798), while the comedies of Ivan Krylov, better known for his verse fables, and Vladimir Lukin, also played an important role in establishing a native Russian tradition.

However, few plays from that era have remained in the repertoire, and Fonvizin's *The Minor* was almost the only eighteenth-century Russian play regularly staged in the Soviet period. Nevertheless, by the time Gogol came to the theatre in the 1830s, a substantial body of drama had been created, distinctively Russian, despite its debt to French models. In fact, Molière remained influential in Russia long after he had gone out of fashion in France, supplanted by sentimental *comédies larmoyantes*, under the impact of Rousseau and the cult of sensibility. Russian dramatists produced their fair share of such

things, and indeed learned much from them, but
Molière's didacticism, the Classical impulse to ridicule
fools and knaves, remained strong in Russia, and is the
driving force behind Aleksandr Griboedov's *Woe From
Wit* (1824).

Griboedov's brilliant verse satire is an attack on the
obscurantism of Moscow society in the 1820s, seen
through the eyes of the hero Chatsky, recently returned
from abroad. For his pains, of course, Chatsky is
dismissed as a madman, and the author faced little
better. Submitted to the censor, the play was instantly
banned, and became known only through private
readings and *samizdat* copies – though it is said that the
latter ran into several thousand. Griboedov died
tragically young, killed by Muslim fanatics in Teheran,
and *Woe From Wit* was not performed in full until 1869,
some thirty years after his death. Pushkin's *Boris Godunov*
(1825), and Lermontov's *Masquerade* (1835), similarly fell
victim to the regime's determination to stifle independent
thought.

In terms of sheer output, however, Russian theatre
was already booming by the 1820s, and the public's
appetite for vaudevilles, in particular, seemed
inexhaustible. These lightweight offerings, the forerunners
of modern musical comedy, combined elegant, witty
dialogue with song and dance, and while Gogol
considered them shallow, escapist entertainment, he
undoubtedly learned from them. The tradition of
Molière, with its seriousness of purpose, was too overtly
didactic, while the vaudevilles were pacy and sparkling,
with no long passages of instruction to impede the flow.
Gogol had no quarrel with the didactic in principle; on
more than one occasion he likened the stage to a lectern
or pulpit from which an improving lesson could be read
to the world, but the mode of delivery was a vexed
question. The comic integrity of both *The Minor* and *Woe
From Wit*, for example, is flawed by a perceived necessity
to spell out the nature of virtuous conduct, to counter

the images of knavery and folly from which the plays draw their strength. Gogol, though he approved of Fonvizin and Griboedov's serious intent, chose a very different path.

Gogol's literary career was relatively short – little more than a decade, and the latter part of it spent revisiting earlier work, rewriting, or reflecting on its significance, in the light of his increasing preoccupation with spiritual concerns. As a proportion of his creative output, accordingly, his three completed plays, and a handful of fragments, are as important as his novels and short stories, and as carefully crafted.

Gogol's achievement was not to create new forms; indeed, in the main, his characters are conventional types and his plots are well worn. Both *The Government Inspector* and *The Gamblers*, for example, are comedies of mistaken identity, and *Marriage* is basically a variation on the theme of true love thwarted. In terms of construction, moreover, they are 'classical' almost to a fault, observing the unities of time, place and action with remarkable assiduity. And despite their detailed realism, their sheer 'Russianness', expressing Gogol's personal credo, they draw sustenance from the Aristophanic concept of theatre as microcosm, in which the permanent, universal traits of human folly are exposed to ridicule.

Discounting his dramatised afterthoughts to *The Government Inspector*, Gogol made six attempts at writing for the theatre, beginning with a satire, *The Order of St Vladimir, Third Class*, in 1832, of which only four discrete scenes remain, now mainly of interest for the light they shed on Gogol's later work. His reported scheme for the play was to present a bureaucrat so obsessed with obtaining the decoration (which conferred nobility on the recipient), that he finally loses his sanity, and believes that he himself has metamorphosed into the coveted medal – suggesting parallels with both *Diary of a Madman* and *The Nose*. However, the best of these

surviving scenes, as Gogol later revised them for his
Collected Works, is 'A Fragment', which concerns a
social-climbing mother's efforts to marry off her
unwilling son – a theme dear to Gogol's heart. Though
not without merit, and occasionally performed, they are
apprentice work, and it is difficult to imagine how Gogol
might have woven their various plot-lines together. As it
was, he realised there was no likelihood of it passing the
censor, and duly abandoned it.

Gogol's next dramatic venture, *The Suitors*, begun in
1833, contained little to trouble the censor, but it took
nine years, and some radical revision, before it surfaced
eventually as *Marriage* in 1842. In its original form, the
plot was relatively straightforward: a noblewoman
employs a matchmaker to find her a husband; four
suitors duly arrive, insult each other, and offer to marry
her; she, however, is so dazzled by their attentions that
she accepts all four – at which point Gogol set the play
aside, to be swiftly overtaken by *The Government Inspector*.

Gogol had in fact sent Pushkin a copy of *The Suitors*
in 1835, some time before his request to the poet for
the 'authentic Russian anecdote', out of which he
would create his great comic masterpiece. Not
surprisingly, perhaps, in the turmoil that followed the
first performances of *The Government Inspector*, Gogol was
in no haste to resume work on the earlier play, and the
version finally printed, in his Collected Works of 1842,
and staged in St Petersburg in December of that year,
differed markedly from the original.

Where *The Suitors* was set in the provinces, the action
of *Marriage* takes place in St Petersburg. And while the
bones of Gogol's first thought, rival suitors and giddy
would-be bride, remain largely intact, an entirely new
plot, too prominent to be termed a sub-plot, has been
introduced, along with new characters to enact it.
Podkolyosin, the hero, is a St Petersburg civil servant
contemplating marriage, prompted more by duty, or
perhaps fashion, than any genuine desire to abandon his

comfortable bachelor existence. His wavering purpose is shored up by the insistent urgings of his friend Kochkaryov, who acts as an amateur matchmaker, competing with, and finally outdoing, the professional whose services Podkolyosin has engaged.

These two focus the action of *Marriage*, from its opening scene, with Podkolyosin's absurd role-playing of a man about to be wed, to its conclusion, when after Kochkaryov's best efforts, and a touching little soliloquy on domestic bliss, Podkolyosin takes cold feet and leaps out of the first-floor window. There is a manic edge to Kochkaryov which is typically Gogolian, and apart from the fact that he himself is unhappily married, there seems no reason why he should be so committed to finding a wife for his friend. Gogol integrates his parallel plots very smoothly, however, and Kochkaryov's scheming on Podkolyosin's behalf, to wreck the prospects of the other suitors, adds much to the comic suspense.

Gogol's jaundiced view of marriage is well documented, as is his dislike of the conventional comedies of his own day, with their stereotyped happy endings – young lovers united in wedlock, all obstacles at last overcome. Ironically, *Marriage* starts out by conforming to that pattern: the love action is central; its progress is obstructed throughout, in a variety of ways; but at the point of a happy ending it stands that convention on its head. The extent of Gogol's radical overhaul of the genre is thus obvious enough, and it is significant that not one of his would-be marrieds is motivated by love. Even the heroine, Agafya, more conventionally attractive than her precursor in *The Suitors*, sees marriage in terms of advancing her social position, and although herself the daughter of a merchant, she is prepared to wed any of her gentlemen suitors, *except* the lone merchant, Starikov, whose motives are incidentally the least tainted. Omelet, for example, is more interested in the inventory of Agafya's possessions, than her person; Anuchkin, without the faintest idea why, needs a wife who can speak French – her other attributes scarcely matter; Zhevakin, the retired naval officer, is at least physically attracted to Agafya, but his generalised lust more resembles an itch picked up in foreign climes, a kind of relapsing fever, and has very little to do with love. Gogol's view of the family is equally bleak, and Podkolyoskin himself is hardly enchanted by the picture Kochkaryov paints of a whole brood of spitting-image Podkolyosins, miniature bureaucrats in the making.

Like all Gogol's comedy, *Marriage* has a dark undertow, but it can easily be read as old-fashioned critical realism, a well-aimed hit at the St Petersburg minor nobility and their pretensions. That does scant justice to a complex and intricately constructed piece, whose little gallery of grotesques, with their detailed tics and manic chatter, are not only witless, but soulless, hollow to the core.

Strangely, Gogol himself seems to have undervalued the play, showing little interest in its first peformance, perhaps wisely, since it was by all accounts hissed off stage, by an audience expecting Podkolyosin to return and deliver the kind of happy ending to which they were accustomed. At any rate, neither *Marriage* nor *The Gamblers*, which existed in draft form at least before 1836, has had anything like the success of *The Government Inspector*, in Russia or abroad.

In the case of *The Gamblers*, the fact that Gogol himself consigned the play to Volume IV of his Collected Works, among sundry dramatic fragments, suggests a lack of confidence in his own creation, but its continuing neglect is surely unjustified. On the surface, it is more purposefully plotted than the other two, in the sense that the outcome, albeit unexpected, is the consequence of a declared plan, set in motion by a professional cardsharp, Ikharev. The fact that he himself becomes the victim of an elaborate 'sting', as his scheme rebounds on him, gives the play a satisfying shape, but in the view of some critics that is its main weakness. Gogol's characters in general act without forethought, casual opportunists, like Khlestakov in *The Government Inspector*, who exploits his good fortune with only the haziest understanding of its cause.

Indeed, one of the most persistent early criticisms of the latter play was its apparent lack of plot, which Gogol defended himself against by arguing that the mainspring of his comedy was a controlling *idea*, rather than the will of any individual. Khlestakov thus has his impersonation thrust upon him, by the collective fear and guilt of the officials, and any other reading misses the point of the satire, which is that the situation arises from the very nature of a corrupt society.

That element of spontaneity is largely missing from *The Gamblers*, and the presence of a clear plot invites questions of motivation, probability, and suchlike. One difficulty concerns the fact that some of the tricksters never emerge from behind their masks, so that their characterisation appears shallow, and the audience, like Ikharev himself, has to take them at face value. Even at that, the counterfeit 'marks', old man Glov, the upright and indulgent father, and his spendthrift, cavalry-obsessed son, should have fooled no one, least of all an artist like Ikharev.

The Gamblers has also been criticised for its cynicism; there is nothing positive to be gleaned from the play, even by implication; virtue fails to triumph, because there is none, and vice walks off unscathed; Uteshitelny and his gang are simply smarter than Ikharev, artists of superior talent. Gogol's plays are determinedly free of messages, however, and when his opponents attacked *The Government Inspector* for showing not a single intelligent or virtuous character, more astute critics argued that the author's own intelligence and virtue were patent throughout.

These qualities are perhaps less in evidence in *The Gamblers*, but the theme itself has a distinguished history

in Russian literature, and many writers, including
Pushkin, Lermontov, and Dostoevsky, have plumbed the
metaphorical depths of the card-table. In Gogol, as
elsewhere, wealth and penury, life and death, hang on
the turn of a card; trust in divine providence is replaced
by surrender to blind chance. Cheating is elevated to the
status of an art, perfected by years of study; the polite
forms of human intercourse conceal dog-eat-dog
predation; comradeship, of the sort Uteshitelny and his
companions invite Ikharev to share, is an expedient,
the co-operative strategy of the pack animal.

Relationships between the sexes are unproductive in
Gogol generally, but it is significant that the only female
presence in *The Gamblers*, Ikharev's adored 'Adelaida
Ivanovna', is a marked deck of cards, and the nearest
approach to a family is that of the boy card-sharp, whose
story parodies the infancy of Christ, with crowds coming
from miles around to witness his miracle-working.
Gogol's deceptively simple plot mechanism, of the biter
bit, is also a vehicle for the exploration of fundamental
questions of identity; its setting, in a provincial tavern, is
like an ante-room to hell, occupied by the already-dead,
as far as any human warmth is concerned. Certainly it is
amusing – Gogol's eye and ear for the grotesque remain
pin-sharp, but the laughter this clever and under-rated
little comedy invites is distinctly sardonic.

All three of Gogol's plays are in some form or other
the product of his St Petersburg years, but *Marriage* and
The Gamblers were not staged until the early 1840s, long
after the remarkable success of *The Government Inspector*,
and the furore that attended it, had driven him into self-
imposed exile. Although the details are obscure at points,
there is no doubt that Pushkin did furnish Gogol with
the Russian anecdote he requested, an account of a civil
servant masquerading as an important official in a
provincial town in Bessarabia. Pushkin himself had a
similar experience in the Orenburg region in 1833,
gathering material for his history of the Pugachov

rebellion, but the notion of an incognito traveller reporting on the citizenry is scarcely original in a Russian context, fact or fiction.

Gogol might have drawn on a number of literary models, among them Nikolai Polevoy's comedy *The Government Inspectors* (1832), which revolves around the idea of the threatened townsfolk attempting to suborn the officials with various bribes and sweeteners, matched to their known weaknesses. Also Grigory Kvitka's *A Visitor from the Capital* (subtitled *Uproar in a Provincial Town*), although not published until 1840, was written in 1827, and Gogol almost certainly knew the work of his fellow-Ukrainian. In outline, Kvitka's main action is remarkably similar to Gogol's, but the differences are significant; Kvitka takes most of the first act, for example, to deliver the stunning blow with which Gogol's play opens. And the generally slow pace of *A Visitor from the Capital* is not aided by a sub-plot developing a conventional love intrigue, of the sort Gogol roundly detested. Again, in keeping with the didactic tradition, Kvitka feels constrained to spell out the nature of good government, something which Gogol determinedly rejects.

Not the least remarkable fact about *The Government Inspector* is the speed at which Gogol wrote it. Between his famous begging letter to Pushkin, of 7 October 1835, and another letter, to his journalist friend Pogodin, announcing the completion of his new comedy, less than two months elapsed, and a few weeks later, on 18 January, Gogol read the play aloud to a select group of friends, including Pushkin, at the poet Zhukovsky's house. At a time when dramatic works had to be licensed by two different censors – one controlling publication, the other performance, and neither distinguished for speed of response – Gogol's masterpiece was approved for production by the Tsar himself, and premièred in St Petersburg on 19 March 1836.

Why Nicholas I authorised *The Government Inspector* for

performance remains a mystery, although Zhukovsky, as tutor to the heir apparent, had privileged access to the Tsar, and no doubt argued its merits persuasively. However, Nicholas' dealings with the leading writers of the period were in general extremely high-handed, and Pushkin, Küchelbecker, and Lermontov all endured persecution during his reign, ranging from major restrictions on their liberty to petty interference. *Boris Godunov*, for example, was not simply banned from performance; acting under advice from Pushkin's literary enemies, Nicholas even patronisingly suggested that the poet should rewrite his play as a historical novel in the manner of Sir Walter Scott.

Gogol's treatment was thus privileged indeed, and it cannot be explained by his own reactionary commitment to the autocracy, which he made public only much later, in his 1846 collection of essays, *Selected Passages from Correspondence with Friends*, much to the dismay of the Russian liberal intelligentsia. The most likely explanation for Nicholas' untypical action is that, like most dictators, he enjoyed watching his subordinates squirm, but one must question his judgement if he imagined that the political fall-out from Gogol's masterpiece would be easily contained.

Gogol took a keen interest in the Aleksandrinsky Theatre production, regularly attending rehearsals and offering advice, which the actors predictably ignored. Dür, for example, played Khlestakov as a stereotype trickster, wholly misrepresenting Gogol's intention, and in general the play was performed as farce. Despite that, enough of Gogol's satire eventually got through to divide the audience along clear political lines and *The Government Inspector* became an instant *cause célèbre*. Tsar Nicholas is said to have laughed very heartily, and remarked that, 'Everyone gets his come-uppance, not least myself', but his loyal supporters in the right-wing press, Bulgarin of *The Northern Bee*, for example, vilified Gogol, accusing him of slandering Russia, while another critic even called for him to be exiled to Siberia.

The Government Inspector presented a challenge to its first
audience in a number of respects. Hostile reviewers
complained of its feeble plot, and in the sense of a
purposeful action taking shape from the characters'
motivation, this is true. Gogol's people simply respond to
the situation they find themselves in, Khlestakov
included, and the obligatory 'positive' character, focusing
the audience's comfortable prejudices, is also absent.
Even the victims of the Mayor's corrupt dealings,
arguing their several cases to the bogus Inspector, are
rather unsympathetic, and as a complication of the main
narrative of mistaken identity, they are little more than a
sideshow. The love interest, moreover, which in Gogol's
absurd parody has Khlestakov propositioning both the
Mayor's wife and daughter, was a particular focus of
criticism, with Bulgarin likening their behaviour to that
of the savages encountered by Captain Cook in the
Sandwich Islands. Also, as happened with the first
staging of *Marriage*, many in the audience expected the
hero to return and do the decent thing. How else was a
comedy supposed to end, after all? However, though the
celebrated final *tableau vivant*, which drains the residual
laughter from the play, was added only later, Gogol's
comedy showed scant regard for the conventions of
the day.

For its formal innovations alone, *The Government
Inspector* was certain to arouse controversy, but its
depiction of a provincial authority, charged with
dispensing justice, education, health care, etc., by the
Tsar of All the Russias, yet rotten to its very core,
virtually exploded on the public consciousness. Gogol
claimed to be surprised at the reaction, but as he well
knew, the Tsarist administration effectively ran on
greased palms, and he might have anticipated trouble
from that quarter. Writing to the actor Shchepkin,
however, as the latter was preparing to play the Mayor
in the Moscow production, Gogol complains:

Everyone is against me. Elderly and respectable

> officials cry out, saying that nothing is sacred to me,
> daring to speak like that about civil servants. The
> police are against me, the merchants are against me,
> the critics are against me . . . Now I see what it
> means to be a writer of comedies. The merest hint of
> truth, and not just one person, but the whole of
> society rises up against you.

Ironically, Gogol was if anything more upset by the
support he received from the political left – those who
saw *The Government Inspector* as a long-overdue indictment
of the whole Tsarist regime. As he insisted on a
number of occasions, the target of his satire was
localised abuse of power, not the divinely-ordained
source of that power. That seems rather naive, as if
wholesale bribery and corruption were a mere blemish
on a basically healthy organism, and not the workings of
a systemic poison.

At any rate, Gogol was so disillusioned, both at the
way his play had been travestied in St Petersburg, and
the uproar it had caused, that he refused to attend the
Moscow opening on 25 May 1836, though the new
production was by all accounts much closer to his
intention, thanks largely to the talents of Shchepkin, and
the Moscow reviewers were in general less hostile.
Scandalised or not, audiences flocked to the play in both
cities, and tickets were at a premium. Gogol, however,
affected to believe he was a prophet without honour in
his own country, and had already resolved to leave, as
he told Pogodin in a letter of 10 May:

> I am going abroad to shake off the sorrow that my
> countrymen daily inflict on me. A modern writer, a
> comic writer, a writer dealing with morals and
> manners, should be rather more distant from his
> native land.

For the second time in his career, accordingly, Gogol
fled to the West, travelling first in Germany, Switzerland
and France, before settling down in Rome in the spring

of 1837. For the next twelve years, barring two brief visits to his homeland, Gogol remained abroad, wrestling for much of that time with the complexities, aesthetic and moral, of his great novel *Dead Souls*, but also revising his earlier work, in particular *The Government Inspector*.

In truth, although passages of the play were significantly rewritten – the final dumb show, and the Mayor's famous line to the audience: 'What are you laughing at? You're laughing at yourselves!', for example, were later additions – *The Government Inspector* underwent no radical alteration, nothing comparable to that between *The Suitors* and *Marriage*, say, during the six years prior to its publication in 1842. What did change radically, as Gogol became ever more absorbed with religious and spiritual concerns, was his attitude to the work. There is no hint of any grand design in his letter to Pushkin, the presumed genesis of the play, but Gogol in exile sets in motion a lengthy process of re-interpretation, in which, it must be confessed, he eventually parts company with the vast majority of his audience, then and now.

Gogol's first attempt at clarifying his intention, *Leaving the Theatre After the Presentation of a New Comedy*, published in 1842 but probably written soon after the St Petersburg première, takes the form of a dialogue among members of the audience, overheard by the author himself. Gogol uses the device in the main to answer criticisms already mentioned, concerning the weakness of the plot, for example, and the absence of 'positive' characters. However, he also emphasises his moralising purpose, in a statement about the importance of the right sort of laughter:

> Not the easy laughter which furnishes people with idle diversion and entertainment, but the laughter which wings upwards from man's luminous nature, out of the depths which conceal its eternally surging spring; that laughter which lends profundity to a

subject, forcing things that would slip past us to appear with shining clarity, and without whose penetrating power the triviality and emptiness of life would not frighten us so much.

Misguided criticism accounted for only part of Gogol's disillusionment, however, and around this time he also wrote detailed notes for future interpreters of *The Government Inspector* on how the characters should be performed. Their general drift is to steer the actors away from caricature towards a more subtle exaggeration of 'universally human' personality traits, and it returns Gogol's comedy to the ancient origins of the form, in Aristophanes' concern with society as a whole, rather than individuals.

Character traits are also signposted, throughout Gogol's work, by the use of comic names. The Mayor's, for example, 'Skvoznik-Dmukhanovsky', suggests a draught of air, literally, but has figurative overtones of sharp practice and social climbing; Judge Lyapkin-Tyapkin suggests 'slapdash'; Postmaster Shpyokin a 'snooper'; Constables Svistunov, Derzhimorda, Pugovitsyn, and Police Chief Ukhovyortov derive their names from words meaning respectively 'to whistle', 'to shut one's trap', 'to frighten', and 'to twist an ear'. Khlestakov himself, despatched from the capital, it is believed, to whip these corrupt and indolent provincials into line, recalls a verb whose primary meaning is 'to lash', but as Nabokov observes, a Russian ear also picks up echoes ranging from the swish of a cane to the slap of playing cards.

Gogol's people are thus types, in the very best sense, neither good nor evil, garrulous hyperactive denizens of the human ant-hill, but it would appear that the longer he reflected on the play, the more narrowly Christian that model of society became. In 1846, Gogol wrote *The Dénouement of 'The Government Inspector'*, again in the form of a dramatic dialogue, and offering a fresh interpretation of the work, along lines reminiscent of a medieval

allegory. His provincial mud-hole is now the spiritual
and corporal being of man himself, and the townsfolk
the various passions at war within him. Khlestakov is
man's corrupt conscience made flesh, while the arrival of
the genuine government inspector represents the
awakening of our true conscience at the point of death,
to face the Last Judgement.

Gogol was becoming obsessed with spiritual matters
by this time, and already contemplating a pilgrimage to
the Holy Land. He was also at work on his notorious
Selected Passages from Correspondence with Friends, in part an
apologia for the Tsarist autocracy, in which he not only
defends the institution of serfdom as the expression of
divine will, but argues that the serfs should be kept
illiterate, lest they be infected with liberal ideas. Not
surprisingly, those same left-wing critics who had so
enthusiastically welcomed his *Government Inspector* ten years
earlier, now rounded on him in fury. Belinsky, the most
eloquent of them, wrote to Gogol from Saltzbrunn,
denouncing him as

> ... the preacher of the knout, the apostle of
> ignorance, the advocate of obscurantism and
> superstition, the panegyrist of Tartar morals ...

and suggesting he was either sick, in urgent need of
treatment, or else mad. Belinsky's letter incidentally went
on to achieve its own fame among the intelligentsia, and
a few years later, Dostoevsky's 'crime' of reading a copy
aloud at an underground debating society cost him his
liberty, and very nearly his life.

At any rate, Gogol's revisionist stance towards his
earlier work also failed to impress his friends in the
theatre. Shchepkin, for example, in response to Gogol's
request that he should perform *The Dénouement*, flatly
refused, and indeed it must have seemed a bizarre
suggestion, from a writer who had done so much to
liberate Russian comedy from its traditional clumsy
didacticism. Towards the end of his life, while he

agonised over a sequel to *Dead Souls*, Gogol is believed
to have contemplated rewriting *The Government Inspector*,
but the version published in his Collected Works of 1842
fortunately remains the definitive text, though it was not
peformed in full until 1870.

Gogol's work was dogged by controversy almost from
the moment it was written, and the history of its
interpretation reflects that. In his own lifetime, though it
was in general treated as farce by actors literally out of
their depth, *The Government Inspector* became a proving
ground for the kind of meticulously detailed realism, in
the performances of Shchepkin, for example, without
which the comedies of Ostrovsky, a generation later,
would have been inconceivable. By that time, Gogol had
achieved the status of revered classic, but the tendency
was to play his work as a period piece, focusing on the
modes and manners of a bygone age.

Towards the end of the century, Gogol as social
realist gave way to Gogol as proto-Symbolist,
accompanied by a marked shift in attitudes towards
Khlestakov. In Gogol's own day, the Mayor was
regarded as the leading role, not by the playwright, it
must be said, but the interpretation of Gogol's 'innocent'
deceiver is crucial to the audience's understanding of the
piece. Khlestakov hovers between real and unreal, an
apparition materialising in the townspeople's
consciousness out of the dank, foggy streets of St
Petersburg, the phantasmagorical city of Pushkin, Gogol,
Dostoevsky and Bely. Symbolist critics even saw
Khlestakov as the Devil incarnate, a new twist, perhaps,
on the allegorical reading of the play proposed by Gogol
in his *Dénouement*.

Russian productions of *The Government Inspector* this
century have tended to swing between these two
extremes. The psychological realism of Stanislavsky was
the driving force behind a notable revival at the Moscow
Art Theatre in 1921, in which Mikhail Chekhov,
nephew of Anton, played Khlestakov as part clown, part

pathological liar, emphasising the spiritual vacuity of the
character underlying the manic energy. During the later
Soviet period, predictably, the view of Gogol as critical
realist prevailed, but before the darkness descended, with
Stalin's brutal suppression of all creative thought,
Meyerhold's staging of *The Government Inspector* in 1926
was hailed as the first truly 'Gogolian' production of the
play, and is still seen as representing a benchmark.

Meyerhold's lavish production employed a much-
expanded text, with additional material from other
Gogol works, including *Dead Souls* and *The Gamblers*, and
an important element of music. Gogol's five acts were
re-fashioned as fifteen episodes, and the set was
dominated by a vast sweep of mahogany doors, through
which disembodied hands were thrust, for example,
during the bribery scene. Khlestakov's first entry, dressed
all in black, with a stovepipe hat and sinister-looking
spectacles, suggested a Symbolist reading, as did the
concluding scene, in which the townspeople joined hands
and made their exit through the audience, led by a
fiddler, like a medieval Dance of Death. The curtain
then parted to reveal an array of life-sized effigies, posed
as Gogol had directed for the final *tableau vivant*, the
'dead souls', as it were, of Meyerhold's powerful
metaphor of Imperial Russia.

Though Gogol held strong views about how his work
should be understood, his dramatic method has ensured
that the plays themselves, while bursting with characters
talking their heads off, maintain a discreet silence on the
subject. That is to say, like all great art, they are wiser
than their creator, and in that respect it may be
illuminating finally to counterpose two views on Gogol's
achievement. In *An Author's Confession*, published after his
death, Gogol himself declares:

> In *The Government Inspector* I resolved to gather into one
> heap everything that was bad in Russia, which I was
> aware of at that time, all the injustices being
> perpetrated in those places, and in those

circumstances that especially cried out for justice, and tried to hold them all up to ridicule, at one fell swoop. However, as is well known, that produced a tremendous effect. Through the laughter, which I had never before vented with such force, the reader could feel my deep sorrow.

Vladimir Nabokov, who regards *The Government Inspector* as the greatest play in the Russian language, writing in 1944, begs to differ:

Gogol's play is poetry in action, and by poetry I mean the mysteries of the irrational as perceived through rational words. True poetry of that kind provokes – not laughter and not tears – but a radiant smile of perfect satisfaction, a purr of beatitude.

Stephen Murline, 1999

The Government Inspector

If your face is twisted, it's no use blaming the mirror.
— Popular saying

Characters

Skvoznik-Dmukhanovsky, **Anton**, *a provincial mayor*
Anna, *his wife*
Marya, *his daughter*
Khlopov, *Superintendent of Schools*
Khlopov's wife
Lyapkin-Tyapkin, *a judge*
Zemlyanika, *Charities Warden*
Shpyokin, *Postmaster*
Dobchinsky ⎱ *local landowners*
Bobchinsky ⎰
Khlestakov, *a St Petersburg clerk*
Osip, *his manservant*
Gibner, *the district physician*
Lyulyukov
Rastakovsky ⎱ *retired civil servants and local dignitaries*
Korobkin ⎰
Korobkin's wife
Ukhovyortov, *Chief of Police*
Svistunov
Pugovitsyn ⎱ *constables*
Derzhimorda ⎰
Abdulin, *a merchant*
Poshlyopkina, *a locksmith's wife*
Mishka, *the Mayor's manservant*
A sergeant's widow
A waiter at the inn
Guests, merchants, townsfolk, petitioners
A gendarme

Notes to the Actors:
Characters and Costumes

The Mayor: a man grown old in the service, and in his own way extremely shrewd. Despite his bribe-taking, he conducts himself with dignity; grave in demeanour, even rather sententious; speaks neither loudly or softly, neither too much nor too little. His every word is significant. His features are coarse and hard, someone who has worked his way up from the ranks. Rapid transitions from fear to joy, from servility to arrogance, reveal a man of crudely developed instincts. Routinely dressed in official uniform, with braided facings, top-boots and spurs. Short grizzled hair.

Anna Andreevna: his wife, a provincial coquette of a certain age, educated partly out of romantic novels and album verse, and partly from bustling around, overseeing the pantry and the maids' room. She is extremely inquisitive and displays her vanity at every turn. Occasionally has the upper hand over her husband, but only when he is stuck for a reply, and her dominance extends no further than trivial matters, expressed in nagging and mockery. She has four complete changes of costume in the course of the play.

Khlestakov: a young man of about twenty-three, slim-built, almost skinny; a little scatterbrained, with, as they say, not a great deal upstairs; one of those people in government service referred to as 'nitwits'. Speaks and acts without a thought. Quite incapable of concentrating on any particular idea. His delivery is rather staccato, and he says the first thing that comes into his head. The more naivety and simplicity the actor brings to his role, the more successful he will be. Dressed in the height of fashion.

Osip: his manservant, like the generality of servants who are getting on in years: sober-sided, eyes downcast most of the time; something of a moraliser, fond of repeating little maxims to himself, but for the benefit of his master. His voice is almost always level, but in conversation with Khlestakov, occasionally takes on a harsh, abrupt tone, to the point of rudeness. He is more intelligent than his master, and thus quicker on the uptake, but doesn't say much, and craftily keeps his own counsel. Wears a shabby grey or dark blue coat.

Bobchinsky and **Dobchinsky**: both men are short and squat and intensely inquisitive; their resemblance to one another is quite extraordinary; both have little pot-bellies, both gabble at high speed, helped along by gestures and hand-waving. Dobchinsky is slightly taller and more sedate than Bobchinsky, but the latter is jollier and more animated.

Lyapkin-Tyapkin: the Judge, a man who has read five or six books and fancies himself a freethinker. Much given to conjecture, he weighs carefully his every word. The actor playing him must maintain a portentous expression at all times. Speaks in a deep bass voice, with a drawling delivery, and a throaty wheeze, like one of those antique clocks that hiss before they strike.

Zemlyanika: the Charities Warden, a rather fat, sluggish and cumbersome person, but a sly rogue nonetheless. Extremely servile and officious.

Postmaster: simple-minded to the point of naivety.

The other roles need no explanation. Their originals can be seen almost everywhere. The actors should pay close attention to the concluding tableau. The final lines should produce an immediate electrifying effect on all present, and the entire cast must adopt its new position instantly. A cry of astonishment must erupt from all the women simultaneously, as if from a single pair of lungs. Failure to observe these notes may ruin the whole effect.

Act One

*A room in the **Mayor**'s house. The **Mayor**, **Charities Warden**, **Schools Superintendent**, **Judge**, **Physician**, and two **Constables**.*

Mayor Gentlemen, I have invited you here to inform you of some extremely unpleasant news: we are about to receive a visit from an Inspector.

Judge An inspector?

Warden What sort of inspector?

Mayor A Government Inspector from St Petersburg, travelling incognito. With secret intructions, no less.

Judge Oh dear!

Warden That's the last thing we need!

Superintendent Good Lord! Secret instructions!

Mayor You know, I had a premonition: the whole of last night I kept dreaming about two extraordinary rats. I tell you, I've never seen anything like it: huge, black things, monsters. They came up and started sniffing around, then cleared off. I'll read you this letter, which I've just received from Andrei Ivanovich – I think you know him, Warden. Anyway, this is what he says: 'My dear friend, godfather and benefactor . . . (*Muttering under his breath as he scans the paper.*) . . . to inform you that . . .' Ah, here it is: 'Meanwhile, I hasten to inform you that an official has just arrived with orders to inspect the whole province, and in particular, our district . . . (*Holds up a finger, meaningfully.*) . . . I have this on the most reliable authority, although he is passing himself off as a private citizen. So, as I know you have your little vices like the rest of us, being a sensible chap, who never lets anything slip through his fingers . . .' (*Stops.*) Well, we're among friends here. '. . . I advise you to take

precautions. He may arrive at any time, if indeed he
hasn't arrived already and is staying incognito
somewhere . . . Yesterday afternoon I . . .' Ah, now he
goes on to family business: 'Cousin Anna paid us a visit
with her husband; Cousin Ivan has got very stout, but
can still play the fiddle . . .' et cetera, et cetera. So there
we are, gentlemen, that's the situation.

Judge   Yes, it's a most unusual situation – most
unusual. There's something behind it.

Superintendent   But why, Mister Mayor? What on
earth for? And why us?

Mayor   Why? It's fate, obviously! (*Sighs.*) Until now,
thanks be to God, they've poked around in other towns.
Now it's our turn.

Judge   Well, I fancy we're seeing some quite subtle
realpolitik here, Mister Mayor. I think it means that
Russia . . . Yes, that's it, we're going to declare war, and
the Government, you see, have sent out this official, to
check for treason.

Mayor   Oh, don't be ridiculous! And you're supposed
to be clever? Treason, in this neck of the woods, really!
It's not as if we're on the frontier, are we? Good God,
you could gallop out of here for three years and still not
reach a foreign country!

Judge   No, seriously . . . You don't know . . . I
mean . . . They have some extremely shrewd ideas, the
Government. Distance doesn't come into it, they keep
their eyes peeled just the same.

Mayor   Well, eyes peeled or unpeeled, don't say I
haven't warned you, gentlemen. As you'll see, I've made
certain arrangements in my own department, and I
advise you to do likewise. Especially you, Warden!
Beyond a shadow of a doubt, the first thing any visiting
official will want to inspect is your charity institutions, so
you'd better get them into decent order: clean night-

caps, for a start. We don't want the patients looking like coal-miners, the way they usually go about.

Warden That's all right. I dare say we can stick clean night-caps on them.

Mayor Good. Oh, and hang a notice in Latin or something above each bed – this is your department now, Doctor – the name of the illness, when they took sick, the day of the week and month . . . And it's not a good idea letting patients smoke that foul tobacco so you start coughing and spluttering the minute you go in there. Yes, and you'd better discharge a few: otherwise they'll put it down to bad management or the Doctor's incompetence.

Warden Well, really! Dr Gibner and I have our own system, that's all. As far as treatment's concerned, the closer to Nature the better. That's why we don't bother with expensive medicines. Man is a simple creature: if he's going to die, he'll die; if he's going to recover, he'll recover. Actually, the Doctor would have trouble communicating with them anyway – he doesn't speak a word of Russian.

The **Physician** *utters a sound, mid-way between 'ee' and 'eh'.*

Mayor And I'd advise you, Judge, to do something about that court-house of yours. The watchmen keep geese in the hall, where the clients are supposed to go, and the goslings are getting under people's feet. All right, poultry-farming's a thoroughly respectable business – why shouldn't the watchmen engage in it? But it's not decent, in a court-house. I ought to have mentioned that before, only it slipped my mind.

Judge Fine, I'll have the lot whipped off into the kitchen today. You can come to dinner, if you like.

Mayor What's more, it isn't very nice hanging all sorts of rubbish up to dry in the courtroom, and dumping your riding tackle on top of the document chest. I know you're keen on hunting and all that, but you'd better keep it out of sight for a while. You can hang it back up again, once the Inspector's moved on. And that clerk of yours . . . well, I dare say he knows his job, but he smells as if he'd emerged straight from a distillery – that's not very nice, either. I've been meaning to have a word with you about that too, but I got sidetracked somehow, I don't remember. Anyway, there's surely something he can take for that, if, as he says, it's just his natural odour. You should tell him to eat onions, or garlic, or something. In fact, the Doctor might be of use here, with those medicines of his.

The **Physician** *utters the same curious sound.*

Judge No, he can't get rid of it. He says his nurse dropped him when he was a baby and he's given off a slight whiff of vodka ever since.

Mayor Well, it was just a thought. As far as your internal arrangements go, and what Andrei Ivanovich calls our little vices, what can I say? You know, it's a strange thing, but there's nobody who hasn't got some kind of sin to answer. After all, that's how the good Lord made us, no matter what these freethinkers say.

Judge And just exactly what do you mean by little vices, Mister Mayor? Surely there are vices and vices? I tell people quite openly that I accept bribes, but what sort of bribes, eh? Greyhound pups, that's all.

Mayor It doesn't matter if it's pups or whatever, it's still bribery.

Judge No, not at all, Mister Mayor. For instance, if a certain person accepts a fur coat worth five hundred roubles, and his wife gets a shawl . . .

Mayor Yes, well, you needn't think your greyhound pups'll save you! You don't believe in God, for a start. And you never go to church. At least I've still got my faith, and go to church every Sunday. Whereas you –

you've only got to start talking about the Creation, and it's enough to make a person's hair stand on end.

Judge Well, that's the conclusion I've come to, thinking it out for myself.

Mayor You know, in some cases, too many brains can be worse than none. Anyway, I only mentioned the court-house in passing; I shouldn't think anybody'll want to look in there, frankly. You're lucky with that place, it must be under the Lord's special protection. Now, Superintendent, as overseer of our educational establishments, you'll need to take particular care with the schoolteachers. Of course, they're educated people, they've been trained at all sorts of colleges, but they've got some very strange ways – I suppose they acquire them along with their scholarly vocation. One of them, for instance, that one with the fat chops, I can't remember his name – every time he's up on the platform he pulls the most awful face, like this (*Grimaces.*), and then starts smoothing out his beard, with his hand under his cravat. All right, let him make faces like that at the pupils, that's neither here nor there. Maybe he can't help it, I'm not in a position to say. But you just imagine, if he does that to a visitor, it could be disastrous. This Inspector or whoever might take it personally. And God only knows what might come of that.

Superintendent Yes, but what am I supposed to do with him? I've told him about it often enough. Just the other day, our Marshal happened to drop into his classroom, and he screwed up his face into the most terrifying grimace, like nothing I've ever seen in my life. He didn't mean any harm, I daresay, but I got a dressing-down for allowing our young people to be infected with subversive ideas.

Mayor There's that history teacher of yours, too. He has a good head on him, that's obvious, a positive mine of information, but when he's explaining something he gets completely carried away. I listened to him once – he was fine on the Assyrians and Babylonians, but the minute he reached Alexander the Great, I tell you, it was indescribable. Ye gods, I thought the place was on fire! He ran down off the platform and banged his chair on the floor, full force! All right, Alexander the Great is a hero, but why smash up the furniture? It all comes out of the public purse, you know.

Superintendent   Well, he *is* an enthusiast. I've mentioned it on several occasions, but all he says is, 'Do what you like, I won't spare myself in the cause of learning.'

Mayor   It's like some mysterious natural law: these scholarly types either drink like fish, or else they pull such awful faces you've got to take the holy icons out of the room!

Superintendent   Well, God help anybody in the education business! You're frightened the whole time, people all have to poke their noses in, everybody wants to show they're as clever as you.

Mayor   I wouldn't care if it weren't for that damned incognito! But he'll suddenly pop up: 'Ah, there you are, my dear chaps!' he'll say. 'And who's the District Judge hereabouts?' 'Lyapkin-Tyapkin.' 'Right then, bring me Lyapkin-Tyapkin! And who's the Charities Warden?' 'Zemlyanika.' 'Right, bring me Zemlyanika!' That's the worst part!

The **Postmaster** *enters.*

Postmaster   Gentlemen, gentlemen, tell me, please – what's going on, what's all this about an Inspector?

Mayor   You haven't heard?

Postmaster   Only just now from Bobchinsky. He was in my post office a minute ago.

Mayor Well then, what do you think?

Postmaster What do I think? It's war with the Turks, it must be.

Judge Exactly what I said. Great minds think alike.

Mayor Yes, and fools seldom differ.

Postmaster War with the Turks, definitely. It's the French stirring things up again.

Mayor What are you talking about, war with the Turks? It's us that are going to cop it, not the Turks. We know what it's about − I've got a letter here.

Postmaster Oh well, in that case, it can't be war with the Turks.

Mayor So tell us, Postmaster, what do you make of it?

Postmaster Me? Why me? What about you, Mister Mayor?

Mayor What do you mean me? I've nothing to fear − not much, anyway. Though I'm a bit worried about the business people and townsfolk, of course. They'll say I've been hard on them, but I swear to God if I've taken anything from anybody, there was no malice in it. Actually, I'm beginning to wonder . . . (*Takes the* **Postmaster** *by the arm and draws him aside.*) I'm beginning to wonder if somebody might not have reported me. I mean, why on earth should we get an Inspector? Listen, Postmaster, couldn't you just . . . for the common good, obviously . . . couldn't you just stop every letter that passes through your post office, incoming or outgoing, and well . . . melt the seal a tiny bit? You know, to see if it contains anything like a report, or if it's just routine correspondence? Obviously, if there's nothing in it, you can seal it up again, or deliver it unsealed, for that matter.

Postmaster   Yes, I know, I know. There's nothing
you can teach me on that score. I do it all the time, not
so much as a precaution, as out of curiosity. I like to
know what's going on in the world. It makes fascinating
reading, I can tell you. Some of these letters are a joy
to read, the way they describe events – a real education,
better than the *Moscow Gazette*!

Mayor   So, you haven't picked up anything about
some official from St Petersburg?

Postmaster   No, nothing about St Petersburg, though
there's a lot of talk about officials in Kostroma and
Saratov. It's a pity you can't read those letters, though –
there are some lovely passages in them. There was a
lieutenant the other day writing to a friend, describing
some ball he'd been at, in the most lively manner . . . it
was extremely well done: 'My dear friend,' he says, 'I
pass my life here in transports of delight, young ladies
galore, the band playing, the colours flying . . .' Really,
he described it all with such feeling. I've hung onto that
one deliberately. Would you like to read it?

Mayor   No, there's no time for that. Anyway, if you'd
do me the kindness, Postmaster – anything that turns
up, by way of a complaint or report, don't hesitate to
hold it back.

Postmaster   My pleasure.

Judge   You'd better watch out – one of these days
you'll cop it for this.

Postmaster   Heaven forfend!

Mayor   It's all right, don't worry. It'd be a different
case if you were making any of it public, but this is a
family matter.

Judge   Even so, that's a nasty business you're involved
in. Incidentally, Mister Mayor, I was just coming over to
make you a present of a bitch pup. She's the blood

sister to that dog I've told you about. You'll have heard, of course, that Cheptovich and Varkhovinsky are suing each other now, so I'm in clover: I can chase after the hares on both their lands.

Mayor   Ye gods, what do I want with your hares? I've got that damned incognito preying on my mind. I'm expecting a door to open any second, and wham!

Enter **Bobchinsky** *and* **Dobchinsky**, *out of breath.*

Bobchinsky   Extraordinary occurrence!

Dobchinsky   Unexpected news!

All   What is it? What is it?

Dobchinsky   Unforeseen development. We go into the tavern . . .

Bobchinsky (*interrupting*)   Yes, Dobchinsky and I go into the tavern . . .

Dobchinsky (*interrupting*)   Excuse me, Bobchinsky – I'm telling the story . . .

Bobchinsky   No, no, let me tell it . . . Allow me . . . You haven't got the knack for it . . .

Dobchinsky   You'll get all mixed up, and you'll miss something out.

Bobchinsky   I won't, I won't, honestly! Now, don't interfere, let me get on with it. Gentlemen, please, kindly tell Dobchinsky not to interfere.

Mayor   Look, for God's sake, tell us what's going on! I'm having palpitations here. Sit down, gentlemen! Bring some chairs! Here, Bobchinsky, take a seat. (*They all sit down, grouped round* **Bobchinsky** *and* **Dobchinsky**.) Well, come on, tell us.

Bobchinsky   Please, allow me . . . I'll tell it all in order. Right then . . . just after I'd had the pleasure of leaving your house, sir, when you had been somewhat

troubled, indeed, sir, by the receipt of a certain letter
... well, at that point I dashed off to ... no, don't
interrupt, Dobchinsky! I've got the whole story, sirs,
absolutely all of it. Anyway, as it happens, sir, I hurried
round to Korobkin's place. And not finding Korobkin at
home, I looked in on Rastakovsky, and when I couldn't
find Rastakovsky, why then, I went round to the
Postmaster's, to inform him of the news you'd just
received, sir, and on my way back, I bumped into
Dobchinsky here ...

Dobchinsky (*interrupting*) Yes, near that stall where
they sell the pies.

Bobchinsky Where they sell the pies. Anyway, I
bumped into Dobchinsky and I said to him, 'Well, have
you heard the news our good Mayor has just received in
a letter from a reliable source?' And Dobchinsky had
already heard about it from your housekeeper Avdotya,
sir, who had been sent round to Filipp Antonovich, I've
no idea what for.

Dobchinsky (*interrupting*) A keg of French brandy.

Bobchinsky (*waving him aside*) A keg of French brandy.
So, off Dobchinsky and I go to see Filipp
Antonovich ... Look here, Dobchinsky – don't interrupt,
please don't do that! ... We set off for Filipp
Antonovich's, and on the way Dobchinsky says, 'Let's
drop into the tavern,' he says. 'It's my stomach, I
haven't had a thing since breakfast, my stomach's
rumbling ...' Yes, it was Dobchinsky's stomach at the
root of it. 'They've just had a delivery of fresh salmon,'
he says. 'We can have a bite to eat.' So, we've no
sooner sat down, when this young man ...

Dobchinsky (*interrupting*) Not at all bad-looking, and
in civilian clothes ...

Bobchinsky Not at all bad-looking, and in civilian
clothes, walks into the room, like so, with a sort of

thoughtful, discerning expression on his face – and obviously a lot going on up here . . . (*Taps his forehead.*) Anyway, I have a kind of presentiment, and I say to Dobchinsky, 'Well, sir, there's more here than meets the eye.' Yes, indeed. But Dobchinsky's already signalled to the innkeeper – Vlas, his name is, actually. His wife gave birth three weeks ago, a lively little chap. He'll be an innkeeper just like his father. Anyway, we call Vlas over and Dobchinsky asks him very quietly, 'Who's that young man?' he says. 'Well,' says Vlas, 'That's . . .' Dobchinsky, please don't interrupt. It's not you that's telling the story, so don't keep butting in. You've got a lisp, as I happen to know, and you whistle through your teeth. Anyway, Vlas says he's a civil servant, he says, on his way from St Petersburg, he says, and his name's Khlestakov, he says, headed for Saratov province, he says, and his behaviour's most peculiar: he's been there two weeks already, he says, never leaves the inn, gets everything on tick and won't pay a penny. And while he's telling me all this, it suddenly dawned on me. 'Aha!' I says to Dobchinsky . . .

Dobchinsky No, Bobchinsky, it was me that said, 'Aha!'

Bobchinsky All right then, you said it first, but I said it afterwards. 'Aha!' we both said, Dobchinsky and I. 'Why's he hanging about here, when he's supposed to be on his way to Saratov?' Yes, indeed, sirs. So, there you have it – he's the one!

Mayor Who is? What one?

Bobchinsky He's the civil servant you got the letter about – the Inspector.

Mayor (*in terror*) God almighty, it can't be!

Dobchinsky It's him! He doesn't pay any money, he doesn't go anywhere. Who else could it be? And he's got an official order for post-horses to Saratov.

Bobchinsky It's him, it must be. I mean, he was looking at everything, he misses nothing. He spotted Dobchinsky and me eating salmon – mainly because Dobchinsky's stomach had been . . . well, anyway, he came up and gave our plates the once-over. Put the fear of God into me, I can tell you.

Mayor Lord have mercy on us sinners! What room is he staying in?

Dobchinsky Number Five, under the stairs.

Bobchinsky That's the room those officers had the fight in last year.

Mayor Has he been here long?

Dobchinsky Two weeks. He arrived here on St Basil the Egyptian's Day.

Mayor Two whole weeks! Good God almighty! Take the holy icons out before I start swearing! These two weeks the sergeant's wife's been flogged! The convicts haven't had their rations! The streets are filthy, the whole town's like a dungheap! It's a disgrace! (*Clutches his head.*)

Warden What'll we do, Mister Mayor? March over to the tavern in a body?

Judge No, no! We should send the Mayor in first, the the clergy, then the business community – you know, same as in that book, *The Acts of John the Mason* . . .

Mayor No no, leave it to me. I've got out of some tricky situations before this, yes, and been thanked for my pains. Maybe the good Lord'll get me out of this one too. (*Turns to* **Bobchinsky**.) You say he's a young chap?

Bobchinsky Yes, twenty-three or twenty-four at most.

Mayor So much the better. Young people are easier to size up. It'd be a disaster if it was some old devil –

young people you can read like a book. Right then, gentlemen, make everything ready in your own departments, and I'll go for a little stroll on my own, or possibly with Dobchinsky here – unofficially, of course – to make sure we're not mistreating our guests. Hey, Svistunov!

Svistunov   Yes, sir!

Mayor   Get me the Chief of Police, right away – no, on second thoughts, I need you here. Tell somebody outside to fetch him, and then come back.

The **Constable** *dashes off.*

Warden   Come on, Judge, let's go! We could be in serious trouble here.

Judge   I don't know what you're worried about. Dish out some clean night-caps and that's the end of it.

Warden   What do you mean, night-caps? I was told to give the patients oatmeal porridge, and the stink of cabbage in the corridors is so bad you have to hold your nose.

Judge   Well, that doesn't bother me. Who's going to come into a District Court? And if he looks at any of the paperwork, he'll regret it. Fifteen years I've been on the Bench now, and when I have to consult the Court records, well, I throw up my hands in despair. Solomon himself couldn't sort out truth from fiction in those.

The **Judge**, *the* **Charities Warden**, *the* **Schools Superintendent** *and the* **Postmaster** *all exit, colliding with the returning* **Constable** *in the doorway.*

Mayor   Well, is my droshky ready?

Constable   Yes, sir.

Mayor   Right, go outside and . . . no, wait! Run and fetch my . . . Where are all the others? Are you on your own? I distinctly told Prokhorov to be here.

Where's Prokhorov?

Constable   Prokhorov's at the station-house, sir, but he won't be much use for this business.

Mayor   What do you mean?

Constable   Well, sir, he was dead to the world when they carried him in this morning. They've poured two tubs of cold water over him already, and he still hasn't sobered up.

Mayor (*clutching his head*)   Oh, my God! Look, run outside . . . no, don't, go to my room first, d'you hear? Fetch me my sword and my new hat! Let's go, Dobchinsky!

Bobchinsky   And me too, Mister Mayor, me too!

Mayor   No, no, Bobchinsky, you can't! It's too awkward, we won't all fit in the droshky.

Bobchinsky   Right then, I don't care – I'll run along behind it, I'll just tag along. I only want to peep through a tiny chink in the door, just to see what he's like . . .

Mayor (*to the* **Constable**, *taking his sword*)   Now, hurry and round up all the other constables, and tell them to get hold of a . . . Oh Lord, this sword's scratched! That damned Abdulin – he can see the Mayor's sword's worn out but he can't send me a new one! Honestly, a pack of rogues! Yes, and I bet those swindlers are busy honing up their complaints right now. Anyway, tell the constables to go outside and pick up a . . . dammit, go out on the street, with a brush, right? Sweep the whole street, all the way up to the inn, and make sure it's clean, d'you hear? And you watch out – yes, you! I know you too well – you're as thick as thieves with that lot, you'll be in there, slipping the silver teaspoons down your boot-tops. Just watch your step, I've got sharp ears, you know! What did you do to Chernyaev, the draper, eh? He was giving you two yards of cloth for a tunic, and you whipped the whole roll. So watch it – don't overstep the mark. Right, clear off.

The **Chief of Police** *enters.*

Mayor   Stepan! For heaven's sake, where've you disappeared to? How d'you think that looks, eh?

Police Chief   I've been right here, at the gates.

Mayor   Stepan, listen – there's an official arrived from St Petersburg. What arrangements have you made?

Police Chief   I've done as you ordered. I've sent Constable Pugovitsyn with a squad to clean up the pavements.

Mayor   What about Derzhimorda? Where's he?

Police Chief   He's gone out with the fire-pump.

Mayor   And Prokhorov's drunk.

Police Chief   That's right.

Mayor   How could you let that happen?

Police Chief   God knows. There was a fight outside the town yesterday afternoon – he went to sort it out, and came back drunk.

Mayor   Anyway, listen, this is what you've got to do: Pugovitsyn's a tall chap, you can stand him on the bridge, he'll show to advantage there. And you can pull down that old fence, the one beside the cobbler's shop, and put out some straw markers, so it'll look like a building-site. The more things we pull down the better, it shows the administration's active. Oh, my God, I nearly forgot! There's a mountain of rubbish at the back of that fence, must be about forty cart-loads of it. What a disgusting dump this town is! The minute you put up any kind of monument, or even a plain fence, they pile all sorts of rubbish against it, heaven knows where it comes from! (*Sighs.*) Yes, and if this Inspector asks your police if they're happy, make sure they say, 'Oh yes, Your Honour, couldn't be happier.' Because if anybody's not happy, I'll give them something to complain about afterwards . . . Oh, Lord, I'm a miserable sinner, I truly am! (*Picks up the hatbox instead of his hat.*) But I swear to you, Lord, if I get through this in one piece, I'll light you the biggest candle you've ever clapped eyes on: I'll screw every one of those swines of merchants for a hundredweight of wax. Oh God, oh God! Right, let's go, Dobchinsky! (*Makes to put on the cardboard box.*)

Police Chief   Mister Mayor, sir – that's a box, it's not a hat.

Mayor (*flings it aside*)   Dammit, so it is! And if anyone asks why the church hasn't been built, the one for the Charitable Foundation, the one we received the money for five years ago, then make sure you tell them the building was started, but it burned down. I've sent in a report about it. Only somebody might forget, some halfwit, and say it hadn't even been started. Oh, and tell Derzhimorda not to be too ready with his fists – his idea of law and order is to give everybody a black eye – innocent and guilty alike. Come on, Dobchinsky, let's go! (*Exits, then re-enters.*) And for God's sake don't let those soldiers out in their bare backsides: that garrison's a disgrace, they'll put on shirts and tunics, but they've got nothing on down below.

All exit. The Mayor's wife **Anna**, *and his daughter* **Marya**, *rush into the room.*

Anna   Where are they? Where on earth have they gone? Oh, my God! (*Opens the door.*) Husband! Antosha! Anton! (*Hastily, to* **Marya**.) This is all your doing, you know, it's all your fault. Rummaging everywhere: 'I need a pin, I can't find my scarf.' (*Runs over to the window and shouts.*) Anton! Anton, where are you going? What? He's here? The Inspector? Does he have a moustache? What kind of moustache has he got?

Mayor (*off-stage*) Later, my dear, later!

Anna Later? What use is later? I don't want later . . .
One word, that's all: what is he? Is he a colonel? Eh?
Huh! He's gone! By heaven, I'll make you pay for this!
And this one, the whole time: 'Mama dearest, please
wait for me, I've just got to pin up my scarf, I won't be
a minute.' Huh, so much for your 'minute'! Thanks to
you we've missed everything! Vain creature: the instant
she hears the Postmaster's in the house, she's preening
herself in front of the mirror – first one side, then the
other. She thinks he's after her – yes, well, he pulls a
face every time your back's turned!

Marya Mama, there's nothing we can do. Anyway,
we'll know all about it in a couple of hours.

Anna In a couple of hours! Well, thanks very much,
I'm obliged to you. Why not say a month? That'd be
better still, we'd know even more. (*Leans out of the
window.*) Coo-eee! Avdotya! Eh? What? Listen, Avdotya,
have you heard anything about this newcomer? . . . You
haven't? Stupid woman! He chased you away? So what
if he did, you could've asked him anyway. You couldn't
find out? Huh, your head's full of nonsense – you've got
men on the brain. What? They drove off too quickly?
Well, you could've run after the droshky, surely? Go on,
go on, do it now! Run after them, find out where
they've gone, d'you hear? Find out everything – who
this person is, what he looks like, you understand? Peep
through the keyhole, see what colour his eyes are, if
they're dark or what, then come straight back here this
instant! Go on, go on, hurry, hurry! (*She continues shouting
until the curtain falls, leaving the two women standing at the
window.*)

Curtain.

Act Two

A small room at the inn. A bed, table, suitcase, empty bottle, boots, clothes-brush, etc. **Osip** *is lying on his master's bed.*

Osip Dammit to hell, I'm famished! My stomach's rumbling so much it sounds like a regimental band. We'll never get home at this rate, so what d'you suggest we do, eh? That's more'n a month now, since we left Petersburg. His lordship's been chucking his money around on the road, and now he's stuck here with his tail between his legs, and he doesn't give a damn. He could've hired post-horses, he's plenty of cash, but oh no, not him, he has to make a show of himself every place we stop. (*Mimics him.*) 'Right, Osip, go and find me a room, nothing but the best, mind, and order up the finest dinner on the menu: I can't eat any old muck, I must have the best.' I mean, it'd be a different matter if he *was* somebody, but he's only a jumped-up clerk! Yes, and he gets matey with some fly-by-night, next thing they're at the cards, and he's gambled himself into this hole! God, I'm sick to death of it! I tell you, you're better off in the country: all right, there's no social life, but you've no worries, neither – you get hold of a nice peasant woman, you can spend the rest of your days stretched out on top of the stove, eating pies. Still, you can't argue – when you come right down to it, there's no place like Petersburg. As long as you've got money, you can live like a king – them theatre places, little dancing dogs, anything you've a fancy to. And they talk so refined the whole time, you could be up there with the nobility, near as dammit. You stroll through the Shchukin market, and the traders all shout 'Your Honour!' at you. You can take the ferry-boat, and you're sitting right next to a civil servant, no less. If you fancy a bit of company, you can pop into any shop, and some army type'll tell you all the camps he's been in, or what every single star in the sky means, so you can

practically see 'em, plain as day. Then some old officer's
wife'll drop in, or one of them young housemaids, and
by God, she'll give you such a look – whew! (*Laughs and
shakes his head.*) And the manners of 'em, dammit, they're
so well-bred. You won't hear a single cuss word, and
everybody calls you 'sir'. And when you get fed up
hoofing it, you just hop in a cab and sit yourself down
like a lord – if you don't feel like paying, well, there's a
back door to every house, you can skip out through it
and the devil himself couldn't catch you. Only snag is,
one day you're stuffing your face, the next you're
practically starving, like now, for instance. And it's all
his fault. I mean, what can you do with him? His old
man sends him money, enough to last him a while –
huh, fat chance! Next minute he's out on the town
again, riding around in a cab, and every day it's: 'Get
me a theatre ticket!' till by the end of the week he's
sending me to the flea-market to sell his new frock-coat.
Another time he'll pawn the lot, right down to his last
shirt, so's he's got nothing left but a shabby old jacket
and overcoat. It's the truth, I swear to God! And
nothing but the best English cloth – he'll lay out a
hundred and fifty roubles on a tail-coat, then sell it at
the market for twenty. And don't even mention his
trousers – they'll go for practically nothing. And why's
this, eh? It's because he won't give his mind to his work:
yes, instead of sitting in his office, he's traipsing up and
down Nevsky Prospect, or playing cards. My God, if the
old master knew what was going on! I tell you, he
wouldn't think twice: civil servant or no, he'd whip up
your shirt tail and give you such a thrashing you
wouldn't sit down for a week! You've got a decent job,
so damn well do it! And the landlord's just said he
won't give us nothing to eat till we pay for what we've
had. And what if we can't pay, eh? (*Sighs.*) Dear God,
what I wouldn't give for a bowl of cabbage soup!
Honestly, I could eat a horse. There's somebody at the
door – that'll be him now. (*Hurriedly removes himself from
the bed.*)

Khlestakov (*entering*)   Here, take this. (*Hands* **Osip** *his cap and cane.*) Have you been flopped out on my bed again?

Osip   Now why would I do that? D'you think I've never seen a bed before?

Khlestakov   That's a damn lie. Look at it, it's all rumpled.

Osip   What would I want with your bed? D'you think I don't know a bed when I see one? I've got legs, I can stand. What do I need your bed for?

Khlestakov (*pacing around the room*)   Look in that pouch, see if there's any tobacco.

Osip   Tobacco? That's a laugh. You smoked the last of it days ago.

Khlestakov *continues pacing up and down, pursing his lips into various shapes. Finally he speaks, loudly and resolutely.*

Khlestakov   Right, Osip – now you listen to me!

Osip   Yes, sir – what is it?

Khlestakov (*loudly, but not quite so resolutely*)   You go down there, right?

Osip   Down where?

Khlestakov (*his voice no longer either loud or resolute, but almost pleading*)   Downstairs, to the dining-room . . . And tell them . . . Tell them I'd like a bite of lunch.

Osip   No chance. I'm not going down there.

Khlestakov   What? How dare you, you ignorant lout!

Osip   Even supposing I did go, it'd make no odds. The landlord says he's not giving us no more food.

Khlestakov   Eh? What damnable cheek!

Osip And what's more, he says, I'm going to see the Mayor, he says – that's over two weeks now your master hasn't paid. You and that master of yours, he says, are a right pair of deadbeats, and your master's a nasty piece of work. We've seen your kind before, he says – nothing but riff-raff, the scum of the earth.

Khlestakov Yes, and you're delighted now, aren't you, you pig, telling me all this!

Osip We can't just let anybody come here, he says, and settle themselves in and run up a bill – we'd never get rid of them. I'm not joking, he says, I'm going to the police right now to make a complaint, to have you two flung in jail.

Khlestakov All right, that's enough, you idiot! Now, go and tell him what I said. Damned ill-mannered brute.

Osip Look, I'd better send the landlord up to see you himself.

Khlestakov What? What do I want with the landlord? You go and tell him.

Osip Honestly, sir, it's no . . .

Khlestakov All right, then, damn you! Send the landlord up. (**Osip** *exits.*) God, I'm absolutely ravenous! I went for a stroll, thought it might kill my appetite, but it hasn't, damn it. Yes, and if I hadn't gone on that binge in Penza, we'd have enough money to get home. That infantry captain really took me to the cleaners, he plays a marvellous game of faro, the swine. I couldn't have been sat down for more than quarter of an hour, and he skinned me alive. Even so, I was still raring to have another shot at him. Never got the chance, though. God, what a miserable dump this is. You can't even get credit at the greengrocer's. It's absolutely disgusting. (*Begins whistling a popular aria, then a folk song, finally anything that comes into his head.*) Well, looks like nobody's coming.

Enter **Osip**, *with a* **Waiter**.

Waiter   The landlord sent me to ask what you wanted.

Khlestakov   Ah, good day, my dear chap! How are you keeping?

Waiter   I'm fine, thanks be to God.

Khlestakov   And how are things in the hotel line? Going well, I trust?

Waiter   Very well, thanks be to God.

Khlestakov   Plenty of guests?

Waiter   Enough to be going on with.

Khlestakov   Listen, my dear chap; they haven't sent up my lunch yet, so if you wouldn't mind hurrying them on a bit – I've some urgent business after lunch, you see.

Waiter   The landlord says you're not allowed any more. And he's going to make a complaint about you to the Mayor's office today.

Khlestakov   What d'you mean complaint? My dear fellow, I've got to eat, you can see for yourself. Good Lord, I'm wasting away here. I'm absolutely starving, I tell you, this is serious.

Waiter   Yes, sir. He said: 'I'm giving him no more lunches, till he's paid for what he's already had.' Those were his very words, sir.

Khlestakov   Well, reason with him, talk him around.

Waiter   And what am I supposed to tell him?

Khlestakov   Explain to him, in all seriousness, that I need to eat. Money doesn't come into it. The man's obviously a peasant – he thinks because he can go a whole day without food, everybody else can. Well, that's news to me!

Waiter   All right, I'll tell him. (*Exits, with* **Osip**.)

Khlestakov   God, this is frightful, if he really won't give us anything to eat. I've never felt so hungry in my whole life. Maybe I could flog some of my clothes? A pair of trousers, say? No, I'd rather starve than go home in anything but my best Petersburg outfit. Yes, what a pity Joachim's wouldn't hire me that carriage in Petersburg – dammit, that would've been something, rolling home in a splendid coach-and-four, driving like a demon up to some neighbour's porch, with the lights blazing, and Osip in livery perched up behind. I can just imagine them all going wild: 'Who is it? What's going on?' And then some flunkey enters (*Draws himself up and mimics a footman.*): 'Ivan Aleksandrovich Khlestakov, from St Petersburg – is Madame receiving today?' These country bumpkins don't even know what 'receiving' means. When some oaf of a landowner pays them a call, he barges straight through to the drawing-room, like a bear. And you can march right up to one of their pretty little daughters: 'Delighted to meet you, I'm sure . . .' (*Rubs his hands together and bows.*) Ugh! (*Spits.*) Oh Lord, I feel sick, I'm so hungry.

Osip *re-enters, followed by the* **Waiter**.

Khlestakov   Well?

Osip   They're bringing lunch now.

Khlestakov (*claps his hands delightedly and jumps up on a chair*)   Lunch! They're bringing lunch!

Waiter (*appears with plates and a napkin*)   The landlord says this is the last time.

Khlestakov   The landlord, the landlord, who cares? I spit on your landlord! Now, what've you got there?

Waiter   Soup and roast beef.

Khlestakov   What? Two courses, is that all?

Waiter That's the lot.

Khlestakov This is ridiculous! I won't accept it. Go back and ask him what he's playing at! This is pitiful!

Waiter Sorry, sir, the landlord says even this is too much.

Khlestakov And what's happened to the gravy?

Waiter There's none.

Khlestakov What d'you mean, there's none? I saw it myself, passing the kitchen, they were making gallons of gravy. And there were two little fat men in the dining-room this morning, tucking into salmon and all sorts of things.

Waiter Well, put it this way, sir, there's gravy, and there's none.

Khlestakov What d'you mean, none?

Waiter Just that, sir – none.

Khlestakov What, and no salmon, no fish, no rissoles?

Waiter For the better class of customer, sir.

Khlestakov What! You ignorant creature!

Waiter Yes, sir.

Khlestakov Listen, you disgusting pig – how come they can eat, and I can't, eh? Why can't I have the same as them, dammit? They're just passing through, same as me, aren't they?

Waiter No, sir, they're different, it's a known fact.

Khlestakov Different in what way?

Waiter The usual way, sir. They pay their bills, you see, that's a known fact too.

Khlestakov Right, I'm not wasting any more breath

on you, you imbecile. (*Ladles out some soup and begins eating.*) Ugh! You call this soup? Dishwater in a cup. It's got no taste whatsoever, and it smells vile besides. I don't want this soup, let me have another sort.

Waiter   We'll just take it back, sir. The landlord says if you don't want it, you needn't drink it.

Khlestakov (*covering his plate with his hand*)   Hold on, hold on – leave it there, you idiot! You might be in the habit of treating your other guests like that, my friend, but I wouldn't advise you to try it on with me . . . (*Eats.*) Ugh, this is revolting! (*Continues eating.*) I don't think there's another person in the world that would eat this muck. Look, there's feathers floating in it instead of chicken fat. (*Cuts up some chicken pieces in the soup.*) Good Lord! You call this chicken meat? Right, let's have the roast beef! Osip, there's some soup left, you take it. (*Begins carving the roast beef.*) And what on earth's this? This isn't roast beef.

Waiter   What is it then?

Khlestakov   God only knows what it is, but it isn't roast beef. They've fried up the kitchen cleaver, it's certainly not beef. (*Eats.*) Damn crooks – look what they give people to eat, eh! One mouthful of this rubbish and your jaws ache. (*Picks his teeth.*) Villains! It's like a hunk of tree-bark, that's what it's like, you can't get rid of the splinters. Two plates of this and your teeth fall out. Scoundrels! (*Wipes his mouth with a napkin.*) Well, isn't there anything else?

Waiter   No, sir.

Khlestakov   Rabble! Scum! If there'd even been a spot of gravy, or a pie. Layabouts – that's all you're good for, robbing innocent travellers!

The **Waiter** *and* **Osip** *clear the table and remove the dishes.*

Khlestakov   Honest to God, it's as if I'd eaten

nothing. Just enough to whet my appetite. If I'd even a few coppers, I'd send out to the market for a bun.

Osip (*re-enters*) The Mayor's arrived! He's downstairs now, asking all kinds of questions about you.

Khlestakov (*alarmed*) I don't believe it! That swine of a landlord must've sent his complaint in already! Oh, my God, what if they really do drag me off to jail? Oh well, I suppose if they treat me like a gentleman, I might . . . No, no, I can't! There are officers and all sorts traipsing around the town, and it's as if it's happened on purpose, I've been putting on airs, and giving some merchant's daughter the eye . . . No, I can't face it . . . I mean, really, how dare he do this to me! Who does he think I am, some wretched tradesman or shopkeeper? (*Draws himself up to his full height.*) I'll tell him to his face, by God: 'Just who do you think you are, eh?'

Someone turns the door-handle, **Khlestakov** *goes pale, and cringes. The* **Mayor** *enters, followed by* **Dobchinsky**, *and stops in his tracks.* **Khlestakov** *and the* **Mayor** *stare at each other, both goggle-eyed with fright, for a few moments. The* **Mayor** *recovers his composure slightly, and comes to attention.*

Mayor Sir, I have the honour to wish you good day.

Khlestakov (*bows*) Not at all, the honour's mine . . .

Mayor And pardon my intrusion, sir, but . . .

Khlestakov Don't mention it.

Mayor You see, sir, it's my duty, as Mayor of this town, to ensure that visitors, and people of rank, are in no way inconvenienced . . .

Khlestakov (*stammering at first, but by the end of his speech, almost shouting*) Well, what can I do? It's not my fault . . . I'll pay the bill, honestly . . . I'll have some money sent from home. (**Bobchinsky** *peeps round the door.*) Actually, the landlord's more to blame than me. Roast

beef he dishes up, and it's as hard as a lump of wood.
And as for the soup – God only knows what he slops
into that, I had to chuck it out of the window. He's
been starving me to death for days on end. And his
tea's most peculiar – it smells more like fish than tea! So
why should I be put in . . . Oh, honestly, I don't believe
this!

Mayor (*meekly*)   Forgive me, sir, it isn't my fault. The
beef I see in our market is always top quality. The
traders bring it down from Archangel, they're sober,
well-behaved people, sir. I've no idea where he gets his
from. But if things here aren't to your liking, sir, well . . .
Perhaps you'll allow me to escort you to another
apartment.

Khlestakov   No, not on your life! I know what you
mean by another apartment – you mean jail! What right
have you, eh? How dare you, sir? Dammit, I'm in
Government service! I'm from St Petersburg! (*Plucking up
courage.*) I'm . . . I'm . . . I'm . . .

Mayor (*aside*)   Oh, my God, he's furious! He knows
everything, those swines of merchants have spilled the
beans!

Khlestakov (*blustering*)   Yes, you can bring a whole
regiment here if you like, I'm not moving! I shall go
straight to the Minister! (*Pounds his fist on the table.*) How
dare you, sir! How dare you!

Mayor (*standing at attention, trembling all over*)   Oh God,
have mercy, sir, don't ruin me! My poor wife, my dear
little children . . . please, don't destroy my life!

Khlestakov   No, I won't have it! This is ridiculous,
what's that to do with me? Just because you've a wife
and kids, I'm supposed to go to jail – that's priceless!

Bobchinsky *peeps round the door, and withdraws in alarm.*

Khlestakov   No, sir – I thank you most humbly, but I

won't have it!

Mayor   It was inexperience, honest to God, sir, that's
all it was – pure inexperience. That, and insufficient
funds . . . You know yourself, sir: a Government salary'll
hardly keep you in tea and sugar, and if I did take the
odd bribe, well, it was the merest trifle – something for
the table, or a bit of cloth for a suit. All that stuff about
the sergeant's widow, the one that keeps the shop, the
one I'm supposed to have had flogged, that's all lies, sir,
I swear to God, that's slander, sir, dreamed up by my
enemies. Oh yes, there's people in this town just itching
to make an attempt on my life!

Khlestakov   So what? I've nothing to do with them.
(*Pensively.*) Look, I've no idea why you're going on about
assassins, or this sergeant's widow . . . A sergeant's
widow's one thing, but if you think you can flog me,
that's a different kettle of fish entirely . . . Damn cheek
of the man! Anyway, I will pay, I'll pay my bill, I just
don't have the money on me right now. That's why I'm
stuck in this hole, because I don't have a single kopeck.

Mayor (*aside*)   Oh, this is a crafty devil! You can see
what he's after, but what a smokescreen he puts up, you
can barely figure him out. You don't know which way
to take him. Well, I'll put him to the test. *Que sera, sera*,
as they say – I'll give it a try. (*Aloud.*) Actually, if you
really are short of cash, or anything else for that matter,
I'm only too ready to be of service. After all, it's my
duty to assist our visitors.

Khlestakov   Yes, do, lend me some money! I'll settle
up with the landlord right now. All I need is a couple of
hundred roubles, maybe even less.

Mayor (*produces a wad of banknotes*)   There we are, sir,
two hundred roubles exactly – don't even bother to
count it.

Khlestakov (*takes the money*)   Well, thanks most awfully.

I'll return this to you the minute I get back to my
estate. I don't put off things like that. Yes, I can see
you're a gentleman, sir. That puts an entirely different
light on the matter.

Mayor (*aside*) Thank God for that! He's taken the
money. Everything'll go smoothly now, I think. And that
was four hundred I slipped him, not two.

Khlestakov Hey, Osip! (**Osip** *enters.*) Call that waiter
back up here! (*To the* **Mayor** *and* **Dobchinsky**.)
Heavens, why are you standing? Gentlemen, please be
seated. (*To* **Dobchinsky**.) Sit down, please, I beg you.

Mayor Not at all, we're happy to stand.

Khlestakov Sit down, do, please. I can see perfectly
well now how open and hospitable you are, but I must
confess, I thought you'd actually come to put me . . . (*To*
Dobchinsky.) Do please sit down!

The **Mayor** *and* **Dobchinsky** *sit.* **Bobchinsky** *peeps
round the door, straining to listen.*

Mayor (*aside*) Might as well go the whole hog.
Obviously wants to preserve his incognito. That's fine,
we'll play dumb too: we'll pretend we haven't a clue
who he is. (*Aloud.*) As a matter of fact, we were just
passing on business, myself and Dobchinsky here – he's
a local landowner – and we purposely dropped into the
inn here, to check that our visitors were being well
looked after, because I'm not like some other mayors,
who couldn't care less. No, sir, not just out of duty, but
pure Christian love for my fellow-man, I want every
mortal soul to have a decent welcome here – and now,
as luck would have it, by way of reward, I have the
pleasure of making your acquaintance.

Khlestakov And I yours, sir. I must confess that if
you hadn't turned up, I might've been stuck here for a
very long time. I had absolutely no idea how I was
going to pay.

Mayor (*aside*) Yes, tell us another one! (*Aloud.*) Sir, if I may make so bold – may I ask in which direction you might be heading?

Khlestakov I'm travelling to Saratov, to my country estate.

Mayor (*aside, with an ironic expression*) Saratov, indeed! And he says it without a blush! Oh yes, this fellow'll take some watching. (*Aloud.*) Well, that's a noble undertaking, sir – travel, I mean. Although they do say it has its pros and cons. It can be a bit of a nuisance, changing horses and the like, but then again, it does broaden the mind. I take it, sir, that you're travelling for your own pleasure, in the main?

Khlestakov No, my father's demanding to see me. The old boy's a bit miffed because I haven't earned myself a promotion yet in Petersburg. He thinks you only have to turn up, and they give you the Order of St Vladimir to stick in your buttonhole. I'd like to see *him* grinding away in some office.

Mayor (*aside*) By God, he can't half spin a yarn, this one! Even dragging in his old dad! (*Aloud.*) Tell me, sir, do you intend a long stay?

Khlestakov I honestly don't know. My father's so damned obstinate, he's like a lump of wood, the silly old fool. I'll tell him straight out: you can say what you like, but I can't live anywhere else but Petersburg. Good heavens, am I supposed to waste away among a bunch of peasants? People want different things out of life nowadays, and my spirit craves enlightenment.

Mayor (*aside*) Fantastic! What a memory! One lie after another, and he never puts a foot wrong. And he seems such a miserable, insignificant creature – you could squash him with your fingernail. Well, sir, just you wait – I'll catch you out soon enough. I think I'll make you tell us a bit more. (*Aloud.*) Yes, you're absolutely right, sir. After all, what can one do at the back of beyond? Take this very town: the sleepless nights you spend, agonising over your country, slaving away, but as for just reward – well, who knows when that'll come? (*Casts her eye over the room.*) Looks a bit damp, this place, don't you think?

Khlestakov   It's a filthy hole – bug-ridden, I've never seen anything like it. Honestly, they bite worse than dogs.

Mayor   Good heavens! A distinguished visitor like yourself, and what's he got to put up with? Good-for-nothing bedbugs, that should never've seen the light of day! I suppose this room's dark as well?

Khlestakov   Pitch dark, yes. Seems the landlord's lost the habit of dishing out candles. So, now and again when I feel like doing something – reading, say, or writing myself, when the fancy takes me – I can't, it's too damned dark.

Mayor   Oh dear, I hardly dare ask . . . no, I can't, I'm not worthy.

Khlestakov   Worthy of what?

Mayor   No, it's too presumptuous of me.

Khlestakov   What are you talking about?

Mayor   Sir, if I may be so bold . . . There's a first-class room you can have in my house, well-lit, quiet . . . No, no, it would be too great an honour, I'm only too well aware . . . Please, don't be angry, sir – God knows, it's a simple heart that offers . . .

Khlestakov   On the contrary, sir, I accept with pleasure. I'll be far better off in a private house, than in this miserable dump.

Mayor   Oh, I'd be absolutely delighted! And my dear wife too! That's just the way I am, sir, I'm a hospitable

man, always have been, especially when it's an
enlightened person like yourself. And don't think I'm
saying this out of flattery. No sir, that's a vice I don't
possess. I'm expressing my feelings, sir, out of a full
heart.

Khlestakov   Well, thank you very much. I can't abide
two-faced people either, I must say. I'm greatly taken by
your frankness and generosity, and I'll freely confess to
you, I demand no more from this life than devotion and
respect. Yes, show me respect and devotion, that's all I
ask.

Enter the **Waiter**, *accompanied by* **Osip**. **Bobchinsky** *peeps
round the door.*

Waiter   Did you wish anything, sir?

Khlestakov   Yes, let's have the bill.

Waiter   Sir, I gave you another bill just now.

Khlestakov   I can't keep track of all your stupid bills.
How much is it?

Waiter   Well, you ordered the set dinner the first day,
then just a starter of smoked salmon the next day, and
after that you had everything put on the slate.

Khlestakov   Idiot! Don't start totting it all up again,
just tell me how much.

Mayor   There's no need to concern yourself, dear sir –
he can wait. (*To the* **Waiter**.) Go on, clear off – I'll
settle up later . . .

Khlestakov   Really? That's very decent of you.

He puts away his wad of notes, and the **Waiter** *exits.*
Bobchinsky *again peeps round the door.*

Mayor   Now, sir, if you'd care to inspect some of our
civic buildings – charitable institutions, workhouses and
such like . . .

Khlestakov What on earth for?

Mayor Well, you'd see how we run things here . . . how we do business . . .

Khlestakov Well, why not? I'd be delighted.

Bobchinsky *sticks his head round the door.*

Mayor Then if you wish, we can go on from there to the district school, to see our methods of instruction in the various subjects.

Khlestakov Yes, by all means.

Mayor After that, if you like, we can visit the town jail and inspect the cells – have a look at how we treat our criminals.

Khlestakov Cells? Why the devil should I want to see them? I'd much rather we inspected your workhouses.

Mayor Whatever you say, sir. Now, how do you intend to proceed? Will you take your own carriage, or ride with myself in the droshky?

Khlestakov I think I'd better come with you in the droshky.

Mayor (*to* **Dobchinsky**) Right, Dobchinsky, that's your seat gone.

Dobchinsky Doesn't matter, I'll manage.

Mayor (*to* **Dobchinsky**, *sotto voce*) Listen, Dobchinsky, run like the wind – as fast as your legs'll carry you, d'you hear? – and take these two notes, one to Zemlyanika at the workhouse, and the other one to my wife. (*To* **Khlestakov**.) My dear sir, I wonder if I might crave your indulgence a moment, while I pen a line or two in your presence to my dear wife, to bid her prepare for the arrival of our honoured guest?

Khlestakov Really, must you? . . . Well, there is ink here, but I don't know about paper . . . Unless you write on this bill?

Mayor Yes, that'll do. (*Writes, and talks to himself at the same time.*) Well, now, let's see how things go after a decent lunch, and a nice pot-bellied bottle of wine! He can have some of our local Madeira – unpretentious, but it'll bring down an elephant. If I could just find out what he's up to, and how far we have to watch out for him.

He finishes writing and hands the notes to **Dobchinsky**, *who makes for the door. At that moment, the door flies off its hinges and crashes onto the stage, bringing with it* **Bobchinsky**, *who has been eavesdropping behind it. General uproar, as* **Bobchinsky** *picks himself up from the floor.*

Khlestakov Good Lord, you haven't damaged anything, I hope?

Bobchinsky Oh no, sir, no – nothing to get excited about, just a little bump on the nose. I'll run over to Dr Gibner's – he does a very good plaster, that should do the trick.

Mayor (*looks daggers at* **Bobchinsky,** *then to* **Khlestakov**) It's a mere trifle, sir. Now, if you'd be so kind as to accompany me, I'll tell your man to bring on your luggage. (*To* **Osip.**) Right, my good man, you're to convey everything to me, at the Mayor's house, anybody'll point it out to you. (*To* **Khlestakov.**) No, no, sir, after you. (*Waves* **Khlestakov** *ahead, and follows him out, but turns round to rebuke* **Bobchinsky.**) Trust you! You couldn't have found somewhere else to collapse? Stretched out on the floor like God knows what! (*Exits, followed by* **Bobchinsky.**)

Curtain.

Act Three

The same room as in Act One. The Mayor's wife **Anna** *and daughter* **Marya** *are standing at the window in the same positions.*

Anna Now look, that's a whole hour we've waited, and all because of your silly airs and graces: she's dressed to perfection, but no, she has to go rummaging some more ... I shouldn't even have listened to her. Oh, it makes me so angry! And there's not a soul to be seen, of course. You'd think they'd all died.

Marya Honestly, Mama, we'll know everything in a minute. Avdotya's bound to appear soon. (*Peers through the window and suddenly shrieks.*) Oh, Mama, Mama! There's someone coming, look, at the end of the street!

Anna Coming where? You see things, that's your trouble. Wait, there *is* somebody – who is it? Quite short ... in a frock-coat ... Who is it? Oh, this is so infuriating! Who on earth can it be?

Marya Mama, it's Dobchinsky.

Anna Dobchinsky my foot – you're imagining things as usual. That's never Dobchinsky. (*Waves her handkerchief at him.*) Hey! You, sir! Come here, quickly!

Marya Mama, it is Dobchinsky, honestly.

Anna You see? You're doing it again, just to be contrary. I'm telling you it's *not* Dobchinsky.

Marya What? Mama, what d'you mean? Look, you can see it's Dobchinsky.

Anna All right, it is Dobchinsky – I can see him now, what are you arguing about? (*Shouts out of the window.*) Oh, hurry up for heaven's sake! You're going too slowly. Come on, where are they? Eh? No, no, you can tell me from there, that'll do. What? Is he very strict? Eh? What about the Mayor, what about my husband? (*Steps back from the window, annoyed.*) The man's a fool! He won't tell us a thing till he's in the room!

Dobchinsky *enters.*

Anna Well, you're a fine one – you should be ashamed of yourself. I was relying on you especially, you're supposed to be a sensible chap, but no, they all suddenly run off, and you follow them! And I still can't get a word of sense out of anybody! Aren't you ashamed of yourself? I was godmother to your little Vanya and Liza, and this is how you treat me!

Dobchinsky Anna Andreevna, I swear to God, I've run so fast to pay my respects to you here, I can scarcely draw breath. My respects to you too, Marya Antonovna.

Marya Good morning, Pyotr Ivanovich.

Anna Well? Go on – tell us what's happening!

Dobchinsky Ma'am, the Mayor's sent you a note.

Anna Well, who is this fellow? Is he a general?

Dobchinsky No, not a general, but not far short. He's so well educated, really impressive manners.

Anna Aha! Then it must be the man in my husband's letter.

Dobchinsky The very same. And I was the first to discover him, along with Bobchinsky.

Anna Well, get on with it – tell us what's happening!

Dobchinsky Everything's going smoothly, thank goodness. He was a bit hard on the Mayor to start with – oh yes, ma'am, he got quite angry, said everything in the inn was terrible, but he wouldn't come here either, and said he wasn't going to jail on the Mayor's account. Then after a bit, when he realised it wasn't the Mayor's

fault, and they'd had a little chat, well, he changed his
mind right there and then, and it all went off
swimmingly, thank goodness. They've gone to inspect
the workhouse and the hospital now ... I'll tell you
straight, ma'am, the Mayor thought there might've been
some secret report on him, and that gave me a bit of a
scare too.

Anna   What've you got to worry about? You're not
even in the service.

Dobchinsky   Yes, I know, but when these bigwigs
start talking, it does give you a turn.

Anna   Oh, don't be ridiculous. That's enough nonsense
– tell us what he looks like. Is he young or old?

Dobchinsky   Young, quite young – about twenty-three
– but he talks just like an old man: 'Very well,' he says,
'I shall see this, and that ...' (*Airily waving his hand.*)
Absolutely the last word. 'I like to do a bit of writing
and reading,' he says, 'but I'm prevented in this room,'
he says, 'because it's a trifle dark.'

Anna   Yes, but what does he look like: is he dark or
fair?

Dobchinsky   No, he's more auburn, and so quick and
sharp-eyed, he's like a fox, it makes you feel quite
nervous.

Anna   Anyway, what does he say in this note? (*Reads.*)
'I hasten to inform you, my dearest, that my situation
appeared grave in the extreme, but trusting in God's
mercy, for two pickled cucumbers, extra, and a half-
portion of caviare, one rouble twenty-five kopecks ...'
(*Stops.*) I can't make this out: what's he talking about,
pickled cucumbers and caviare?

Dobchinsky   Ah, that's because the Mayor had to
write it in a hurry, on scrap paper: that must be his bill.

Anna   So it is. (*Carries on reading.*) 'But trusting in God's mercy, everything will turn out well, I think. Prepare a room quickly for our distinguished guest: the one with the yellow wallpaper; don't concern yourself about another place at dinner, we'll have a bite at the workhouse with Zemlyanika, but do order some more wine; tell the merchant Abdulin to send nothing but the best, otherwise I'll turn his whole cellar inside out. I kiss your hand, my dearest – yours ever, Anton . . .' Oh, my God! We'd better get busy! Right, who's out there? Mishka!

Dobchinsky (*runs to the door and shouts*)   Mishka! Mishka! Mishka!

Mishka *enters.*

Anna   Listen – run over to Abdulin's shop . . . no, wait a minute, I'll make out a list. (*Sits down at the table and begins writing.*) Give this list to Sidor the coachman, tell him to run with it to Abdulin's and bring back the wine. Then tidy up the spare room for our guest, and make sure you do it right. Put a bed in there, a wash-basin and the like.

Mishka *exits.*

Dobchinsky   I'd better run along now, dear lady, see how he's getting on with the inspection.

Anna   Go on, go on – nobody's stopping you!

Dobchinsky *exits.*

Anna   Now, Masha my dear, we'll need to make ourselves presentable. He's from St Petersburg, God forbid he should find something to laugh at. You'd better wear your pale blue dress with the little flounces.

Marya   Ugh! Mama, not the pale blue! I absolutely hate it, the Judge's wife wears pale blue, and so does Zemlyanika's daughter. No, I'd rather wear the one with the flowers.

Anna Flowers! Honestly, you'd say anything, just to be awkward. The blue'll be much better, it'll go with my pale yellow, my little straw-coloured dress, the one I'm so fond of.

Marya Mama, yellow doesn't suit you at all!

Anna Yellow doesn't suit me?

Marya No, it doesn't, I don't care what you say. You need really dark eyes for that colour.

Anna What a cheek! Are you telling me I don't have dark eyes? They're extremely dark. Really, what nonsense you talk. If they're not dark, then how is it, whenever we're telling fortunes, I'm always the Queen of Clubs?

Marya Mama, the Queen of Hearts is more your style.

Anna That's rubbish, absolute rubbish! I've never been the Queen of Hearts! (*Storms out, followed by* **Marya**, *still talking off-stage*.) Honestly, the stuff she comes out with! Queen of Hearts! God knows what she'll think up next!

As they exit, the doors open and **Mishka** *flings out some trash.* **Osip** *enters by another door, carrying a trunk on his head.*

Osip So where's this to go?

Mishka In here, grandad, in here.

Osip Hang on till I get my breath back. God, what a miserable life! This weighs twice as much on an empty stomach, you know.

Mishka So tell us, grandad, will the general be here soon?

Osip Eh? What general?

Mishka Your master, of course.

Osip My master? What gives you that idea?

Mishka   D'you mean he's not a general?

Osip   Oh, he's a general all right, and then some.

Mishka   So what's that? Does that mean he's higher or lower than a real general?

Osip   Higher.

Mishka   Really? So that's why they're kicking up such a fuss.

Osip   Listen, son – I can see you're a smart lad. Do us a favour and get us a bite to eat.

Mishka   Sorry, grandad, there's nothing ready for you yet. I mean, you won't want just any old grub, but as soon as your master sits down to his dinner, they'll dish up the exact same to you.

Osip   Well, what do you call any old grub?

Mishka   Cabbage soup, porridge, pies . . .

Osip   Right, let's have them – cabbage soup, porridge, and pies. Don't you worry, I'll eat the lot. Come on, give us a hand with this trunk. Is there another way out of here?

Mishka   Yes, there is.

They carry out the trunk into a side room. The double doors are opened by two **Constables**. *Enter* **Khlestakov**, *followed by the* **Mayor**, *the* **Charities Warden**, *the* **Superintendent of Schools**, **Dobchinsky** *and* **Bobchinsky**, *with a plaster on his nose. The* **Mayor** *points to a scrap of paper on the floor, and the* **Constables** *rush to pick it up, colliding in their haste.*

Khlestakov   Yes, very fine institutions. I do like the way you show visitors round the whole town. No one ever showed me anything in other places.

Mayor   Well, if I may be so bold, sir – that's because the administrators and officials in other towns are more

concerned with – put it this way – their own advantage.
Here, on the other hand, I may say we have no thought
but how to earn the good opinion of our superiors, by
diligently observing the proprieties.

Khlestakov Lunch was rather decent, I thought. I'm
quite full up. Do you eat like that every day?

Mayor Laid on specially for our honoured guest, sir.

Khlestakov Yes, I do enjoy eating. After all, what's
life for, but to graze among pleasure's blooms? What
was that fish called?

Warden (*scurrying up*) Labberdaan, sir – it's a kind of
salt cod.

Khlestakov It was very tasty. Where did we have
lunch again? The hospital, was it?

Warden That's correct, sir – the charity hospital.

Khlestakov Ah yes, I remember seeing some beds.
So, have your patients all recovered? There didn't seem
that many.

Warden There's about a dozen left, sir, the rest have
all recovered. It's the system we operate here. Since I
took over the running of the place – you'll perhaps find
this incredible, sir – they've been recovering like flies. A
patient's scarcely set foot in the hospital before he's
cured, and not through expensive medicines either, but
good old-fashioned discipline.

Mayor If I may make so bold, sir – the duties of the
chief executive – now, they're fiendishly difficult. I've so
much on my plate, keeping the streets clean, repairs,
putting things to rights . . . I tell you, sir, it'd bamboozle
the cleverest of men, but thanks be to God, it's all
running smoothly. Other mayors, of course, would be
looking after their own interests, but believe it or not,
sir, last thing at night, as I go to bed, I'm still thinking:
'Lord God above, how can I fix it so that the authorities

will see how diligent I am, and be happy with me?'
Whether I'm rewarded or not, well, that's up to them,
but at least I'll be at peace in my heart. After all, if the
town's in good order, the streets swept, the prisoners
looked after, drunks kept to a minimum, what more can
one ask, eh? No no, sir, it's not honours I'm after. They
have their attractions, of course, but virtue is its own
reward.

Warden (*aside*)   That's some yarn he's spinning, the
idle layabout. Talk about the gift of the gab!

Khlestakov   Yes, that's very true. Actually, I do a bit
of serious thinking myself now and again. Sometimes in
prose, but I occasionally dash off the odd verse.

Bobchinsky (*to* **Dobchinsky**)   That's the one, Pyotr
Ivanovich, we're absolutely right. The way he expresses
things . . . he's obviously had a good education.

Khlestakov   Tell me, sirs, do you by any chance have
any sort of amusements, a club, say, where one might
have a game of cards?

Mayor (*aside*)   Oho, my fine fellow, now I see what
you're driving at! (*Aloud.*) Heaven forfend, sir! We
haven't any clubs of that sort, wouldn't hear of them.
I've never picked up a card in my life, wouldn't even
know how to play. I can't bear to look at them, and if
by chance I do catch sight of some King of Diamonds
or whatever, I feel so disgusted I could just about spit.
Matter of fact, I did once build a house of cards, to
amuse the children, and afterwards I had nightmares
about the wretched things. No, God forbid, sir, I don't
know how people can waste precious time on them.

Superintendent (*aside*)   Yes, the swine only took me
for a hundred roubles last night!

Mayor   No no, I'd rather devote my time to serving
the State.

Khlestakov Well, I think you're going a bit far. It all depends on your point of view, doesn't it. For instance, if you're the sort of chap who sticks, when you should treble your stake, well, of course . . . No, don't say that, the odd game of cards can be very tempting.

Enter **Anna** *and* **Marya**.

Mayor Sir, allow me to present my family: my wife and daughter.

Khlestakov (*bowing*) Madam, I'm delighted to have the particular pleasure of meeting you.

Anna And it's even more of a pleasure for us to meet such a distinguished personage.

Khlestakov (*striking a pose*) On the contrary, ma'am – the pleasure is entirely mine.

Anna Oh, sir, how can you? You're only saying that out of politeness. Please, do sit down.

Khlestakov Just to stand near you is happiness enough, dear lady. However, if you absolutely insist, I shall sit down. (*Sits.*) There – I'm sitting beside you, my happiness is complete.

Anna Heavens, sir, I can't believe you mean me . . . I'm sure you must find going *en voyage* in the country most disagreeable after St Petersburg.

Khlestakov Oh, disagreeable in the extreme. One gets accustomed to the *beau monde, comprenez-vous,* and then to find oneself on the road: filthy taverns, a veritable fog of ignorance . . . I will confess to you, ma'am, that if it hadn't been for this *bonne chance* . . . (*Looks round at* **Anna**, *and strikes a pose.*) which has so richly compensated me for all that . . .

Anna Oh, sir, how dreadful it must've been for you!

Khlestakov Anyway, dear lady, at this moment, I am extremely happy.

Anna Goodness, so many compliments. I don't deserve them.

Khlestakov And why in heaven's name not? Of *course* you deserve them, dear lady.

Anna But I live in the country . . .

Khlestakov Ah, but the country has charms of its own – gentle hillocks, shady rills . . . Though naturally it can't compare with St Petersburg. Oh, Petersburg! Now *there*'s a life for you. No doubt you think I'm a mere pen-pusher, but let me tell you, the head of department and I are like *that*! (*Crosses his fingers.*) Yes, he claps me on the shoulder, he says: 'Drop in for dinner, old chap!' I pop into the office for a couple of minutes, just to say: 'Right, do this, do that!' And the copy clerk, miserable rat of a fellow, picks up his pen, starts scratching away. Actually they wanted to make me a collegiate assessor, but I thought, well, what's the point? And the porter comes flying downstairs after me with his brush: 'Sir, sir,' he says, 'please let me give your boots a polish!' (*To the* **Mayor**.) Good heavens, gentlemen, why are you standing? Sit down, please.

The **Mayor**, **Warden** *and* **Superintendent** *all speak together.*

Mayor Sir, we know our place – we don't mind standing.

Warden We're happy to stand.

Superintendent Don't concern yourself, sir!

Khlestakov Gentlemen, don't stand on ceremony – sit down, please. (*They do so.*) I can't abide all that stuff. As a matter of fact, I even try to slip into places incognito. But it's quite impossible, you simply can't hide. I've only got to step outside the door, and it's: 'Look, there he goes, it's Ivan Aleksandrovich!' On one occasion I was even mistaken for the Commander-in-Chief: the soldiers tumbled out of the guardhouse and presented arms. And afterwards their officer – who's a friend of mine in fact – told me: 'You know, we really did take you for the Commander-in-Chief, old boy.'

Anna   Fancy that!

Khlestakov   And I know all the best-looking actresses. I write the odd vaudeville sketch, you see, and I'm pretty well in with the literary types. Yes, Pushkin and I are like that. (*Crosses his fingers.*) I often say to him: 'Well, Pushkin, old chap, how are things? And he'll say: 'Oh, so-so, old boy, can't complain . . .' Yes, he's a real character.

Anna   So you're a writer too? It must be wonderful to be so talented! I suppose you get things into the papers?

Khlestakov   I do, as a matter of fact. Actually, I've written lots of things: *Marriage of Figaro*, *Robert le Diable*, *Norma* – I can't even remember their names. It came about by chance, really – couldn't be bothered writing, but the theatre management kept after me: 'Please, please, old boy, write something for us.' So, I think to myself: 'Well, why not? I'll give it a try.' And that very same night, would you believe, I wrote the whole thing – left 'em all speechless. Yes, I have a quite extraordinary facility of thought. All that stuff you read under the name of Baron Brambeus – 'Frigate of Hope', 'Moscow Telegraph' and so forth – that's mine, you know.

Anna   You're honestly Baron Brambeus?

Khlestakov   Oh yes, I sort out all their articles. Smirdin gives me forty thousand for that.

Anna   Then *Yuri Miloslavsky* must be your handiwork as well.

Khlestakov   Yes, that's mine.

Anna   I knew it, I knew it.

Marya   Actually, Mama, it says on the cover it was written by a Mr Zagoskin.

Anna   You see? I knew you'd start an argument, I knew you would.

Khlestakov   No no, she's quite right. There is one by Zagoskin, but there's another *Yuri Miloslavsky*, and that one's mine.

Anna   Oh well, it must be yours I've read. It's so beautifully written.

Khlestakov   Yes, I must admit I simply live for literature. I have the very first house in St Petersburg, everybody knows it: Khlestakov's house. (*Turns to address them all.*) Gentlemen, if you're ever in St Petersburg, please, please, do me the kindness of calling on me. I give balls too, you know.

Anna   Oh, I can just imagine those balls, they must be magnificent, and so tasteful!

Khlestakov   They're beyond words, ma'am. A watermelon on the table, for instance – seven hundred roubles. Soup shipped in direct from Paris, still in the pot – you lift the lid, and the aroma, well, it's just out of this world! And I'm out at a ball every evening. We get up our little whist party: the Foreign Minister, the French Ambassador, the English and German Ambassadors, and myself. You can practically kill yourself playing cards, you wouldn't believe it. I mean, you run up the stairs to the fourth floor, and you can just about manage to say to the cook: 'Here, Mavra, old girl, take my coat . . .' What am I talking about? I've forgotten I live on the first floor! My staircase alone must be worth, oh . . . And you should see my waiting-room, even before I'm up, it's a sight to behold – counts and princes, all buzzing around, bumping into each other, like a swarm of bees, that's all you hear – buzz-buzz-buzz . . . Now and again the Minister himself . . .

(*The* **Mayor** *and the others rise timidly from their chairs.*) I even get parcels addressed to 'Your Excellency'. I was in charge of the department once too – an odd business, the Director went off somewhere, Lord knows where, and of course, there was a lot of talk about who should take over. Generals and everything volunteered for the job, but when it came to the bit, well, they just weren't up to it. It's not as easy as it looks, by God, it's not! Anyway, there was nothing else for it, they could see that, they had to send for me. So next minute the streets were full of messengers, running all over the place – thirty-five thousand messengers, would you believe! 'What's the problem?' I ask. 'Ivan Aleksandrovich, please, you must take over the department!' Well, I was somewhat nonplussed, I can tell you, standing there in my dressing-gown. I'd have turned it down, but I thought, no, this'll reach His Majesty's ears, and go on my service record besides . . . 'Very well, gentlemen,' I said, 'I accept the post, I'll take it on,' I said, 'only I won't stand for any nonsense, d'you hear? I've got my eye on you lot, so watch out!' And that's just what happened, by God, every time I walked through that department, you'd have thought an earthquake had struck, they were shaking in their shoes, believe me. (*The* **Mayor** *and the others are trembling with fear.* **Khlestakov** *is warming to his task.*) I don't stand for any funny business, no, not me. I put the fear of God into that lot. Even His Majesty's Privy Council's frightened of me. And so they should be. That's the kind of man I am. I don't care who they are, I'll say it to anybody: 'I'm my own man, sir, so there!' I'm here, there and everywhere. I drive to the palace every day. And tomorrow, would you believe, they're making me a Field-Marsh . . .

In his excitement, **Khlestakov** *slips and almost crashes to the floor, but the officials respectfully keep him upright. The* **Mayor** *approaches, trembling from head to foot, scarcely able to speak.*

Mayor B-b-but . . . Y-y-you . . . Y-y-you . . .

Khlestakov (*testily*)   Yes, what is it?

Mayor   B-b-but . . . Y-y-you . . . Y-y-you . . .

Khlestakov (*in the same tone*)   I can't make out a word.
You're gibbering, sir.

Mayor   Y-y-you . . . Your Youness, Your Highness,
please, won't you rest a while? Your room's ready,
there's everything you need.

Khlestakov   Rest? Rubbish! Oh, all right then, I
wouldn't mind a lie-down. Yes, you do a decent lunch,
gentlemen . . . Not bad, not bad at all. (*Theatrically.*)
Labardaan! Labardaan! (*Exits to a side room, followed by the*
Mayor.)

Bobchinsky (*to* **Dobchinsky**)   Well, Dobchinsky,
that's quite a man, eh? That's what you call a man! In
all my born days I've never once been in the presence
of such an important personage – I tell you, I just about
died of fright. What d'you think, Dobchinsky? Where
would you place him as regards rank?

Dobchinsky   Oh, he can't be far off a general.

Bobchinsky   What? A general isn't fit to tie his
shoe-laces! Or if he is a general, he must be the
Generalissimo himself. Didn't you hear the way he
cracked down on the Privy Council? We'd better hurry
and tell all this to the Judge and Korobkin. Goodbye,
Anna Andreevna.

Dobchinsky   Goodbye, dear lady. (*They exit.*)

Warden (*to* **Superintendent**)   Oh Lord, I'm scared
stiff, absolutely petrified. And I don't understand why.
We're not even in uniform. And what's going to happen
when he wakes up and fires off that report to St
Petersburg? (*Exits, deep in thought, followed by the*
Superintendent.) Goodbye, ma'am.

Anna   Oh, what a charming man!

Marya An absolute darling!

Anna But with such a refined manner. You can tell instantly he's a Petersburg type. His bearing, the way he holds himself . . . Oh, it's just wonderful! I absolutely adore young men like that. I could almost swoon. And he obviously took a fancy to me, I noticed that much. He couldn't keep his eyes off me.

Marya Oh, Mama, it was *me* he was looking at!

Anna Oh, for heaven's sake, spare me your nonsense. I've just about had enough for one day.

Marya No, Mama, honestly!

Anna God preserve us, you'd say anything to be contrary! That's enough, d'you hear? What would he want to look at you for? Eh? What earthly reason could he have for looking at you?

Marya It's the truth, Mama, he was watching me the whole time. When he started talking about literature, he glanced over at me, and afterwards when he was telling us about playing whist with the ambassadors, he looked at me then too.

Anna Well, he maybe threw you the odd glance, but just once, if at all. 'Oh yes,' he'll have said to himself, 'I suppose I'd better look at her now.'

Mayor (*entering on tiptoe*) Sshhh . . . sshhh!

Anna What is it?

Mayor I wish I hadn't got him drunk. Suppose even half of what he said is true? (*Thinks.*) And why shouldn't it be true, eh? When a man's half-sozzled like that he gives everything away. *In vino veritas*, as they say. Of course, he'll have embroidered a bit, but if you can't do that these days, you might as well shut up. Good heavens, he plays cards with Ministers and drives to the Palace . . . Honestly, the more you think about it . . .

God only knows what this is doing to my head, it's as if I'm perched on top of a steeple, or waiting to be hanged.

Anna   Well, I didn't feel in the least intimidated. All I could see was a cultured, well-bred young man, the very last word in refinement, and I couldn't care less about his rank.

Mayor   Huh, women! That's typical. It's all one big joke to you, all fuss and feathers! There's no telling what you'll come out with. You'll give the whole show away, and you'll get off with a whipping, while your poor husband cops it. Good God, you've been as free with him as if he were Dobchinsky or somebody.

Anna   Oh, come, you needn't concern yourself on that score. We women know a thing or two. (*Looks at her daughter.*)

Mayor (*aside*)   It's a waste of time talking to you! This is a strange business altogether. I'm still half-dead from fright. (*Opens the door and calls out.*) Mishka, go and fetch Constables Svistunov and Derzhimorda – they're outside the gates somewhere, not far. (*After a brief silence.*) Honestly, the whole world's gone to the dogs. You'd think people would at least *look* the part, but when you get some pathetic, skinny creature – how are you supposed to tell? I mean, you can spot a military man right away, but you put him in a frock coat, and he looks like a fly with its wings clipped. He certainly put up a brave show at the hotel, all those cock-and-bull stories and logic-chopping – I thought I'd never get to the bottom of him. But he caved in at last, and now he's let slip more than he should have. Yes, a *young* man, obviously.

Osip *enters. They all rush up to him, beckoning.*

Anna   Come over here, my dear fellow!

Mayor   Sshhh! Well? Well? Is he asleep?

Osip   Not yet – he's having a bit of a stretch.

Anna   Now tell me, what's your name?

Osip   It's Osip, ma'am.

Mayor (*to his wife and daughter*)   Right, you two, that's enough! (*To* **Osip**.) Now then, friend, are they feeding you properly?

Osip   They are indeed, sir, thank you very much.

Anna   And tell me this – I suppose your master has ever so many counts and princes calling on him?

Osip (*aside*)   What'll I say? If they're feeding me well now, they might feed me even better. (*Aloud.*) Oh yes, ma'am, counts and everything.

Marya   Oh, dear Osip, your master's so handsome!

Anna   And tell me, Osip, please, how does he . . .

Mayor   That's enough, do you hear! You're putting me off with your silly chatter. Now then, friend . . .

Anna   And what rank is your master?

Osip   Well, the usual rank, I suppose.

Mayor   God almighty, will you stop badgering him with your stupid questions! I can't get a word in edgewise. Now, listen, friend – what's your master like? Is he very strict? Does he bawl people out?

Osip   Oh yes, he's a real stickler. Got to have everything just so.

Mayor   You know, I like the look of you. You strike me as a decent chap. Anyway . . .

Anna   Osip, Osip, listen – what does your master wear when he's at home, does he have a uniform, or . . .

Mayor   Will you give over! Honestly, talk about chatterboxes! This is a serious matter – a man's life's at stake here . . . (*To* **Osip**.) Anyway, friend, as I was saying, I've taken a real liking to you. You know, the odd glass of tea never comes amiss, when you're on the road this weather, so here's a couple of silver ones for your trouble.

Osip (*accepting the coins*) Thank you very much, sir, God bless you. You've done a poor man a kindness.

Mayor Not at all, it's my pleasure. Anyway, friend, as I was . . .

Anna Osip, listen to me – what colour eyes does your master like best?

Marya Oh, Osip darling, hasn't your master the sweetest little nose!

Mayor For God's sake, will you let me speak! (*To* **Osip**.) Listen, friend, tell me, please – what sort of things does your master notice? What does he particularly like, when he's on his travels?

Osip Well, that depends. He takes things as he finds them, but he likes to be looked after – the hospitality's got to be top class.

Mayor Top class?

Osip The hospitality, yes. I mean, you look at me, I'm just a serf, but he makes sure I'm treated right, I swear to God he does. We can pay a call on some place, and he'll say: 'Well, Osip, did they look after you all right?' And I'll say: 'No, Your Honour, it was rotten.' 'Ooh, that's bad, Osip,' he'll say, 'I don't like that. Just you remind me when we get back to Petersburg.' But I think to myself, well, what's the odds. (*Waves his hand dismissively.*) I'm a simple man, sir.

Mayor That's good, that's good, that makes sense. Osip, I've just given you some money for tea, so here you are, here's a bit extra for a bun.

Osip I don't know why you're so good to me, Your Honour. (*Puts the money away.*) But I'll certainly drink to your health.

Anna If you come to my room, Osip, I'll give you something too.

Marya Oh Osip, dearest, kiss your master for me!

A faint cough is heard from **Khlestakov** *in the other room.*

Mayor Ssshh! (*Goes on tiptoe, everyone speaks in a whisper.*) For heaven's sake don't make a noise! Now clear off, both of you.

Anna Come on, Masha dear, let's go. There's something I noticed about our guest, but I can't tell you till we're on our own, just the two of us. (*They exit.*)

Mayor Honestly, they'd talk the hind legs off a donkey! They'd give you earache, I swear to God. (*Turns to* **Osip**.) Now then, friend . . .

Enter Constables **Derzhimorda** *and* **Svistunov**.

Mayor Ssshh! You clumsy oafs! Clumping around in those damn boots! My God, you come crashing in here, it's like somebody chucking half-ton weights off a cart! Where the hell have you been?

Derzhimorda Sir, in accordance with instructions, I was . . .

Mayor (*claps his hand over his mouth*) Ssshh! You sound like a damn crow! Caw! Caw! (*Mimics him.*) 'In accordance with instructions!' And that voice, coming up out of your boots! (*To* **Osip**.) Now, off you go, friend, you make sure your master has everything he needs in there. If there's anything we haven't got, just ask. (**Osip** *exits.*) As for you two – stay out on the porch and don't budge! Don't let anybody in, especially not shopkeepers! You let one of those creatures in, and by God . . . The minute you see anybody coming up with a petition, or even if they haven't got one – supposing they just *look* as if they might have a petition – then grab him by the scruff of the neck and kick him out! Like this! Good and proper! (*Demonstrates with his foot.*) D'you hear? Now, ssshh! Ssshh! (*Exits on tiptoe after the* **Constables**.)

Curtain.

Act Four

*The same room in the **Mayor**'s house. Cautiously, almost on tiptoe, enter the **Judge**, the **Charities Warden**, the **Postmaster**, the **Schools Superintendent**, **Dobchinsky** and **Bobchinsky**, all in full dress uniform. The entire scene is played in hushed voices.*

Judge (*organises everybody into a semi-circle*) Gentlemen, for goodness' sake, hurry up and form a circle, let's have a bit more order! God save us, this is a man who drives to the Palace and tears strips off the Privy Council! Get into battle order, come on, line up! No, Bobchinsky, you run around to this side, and you stay where you are, Dobchinsky.

Bobchinsky *and* **Dobchinsky** *both run round on tiptoe.*

Warden It's up to you, Judge, but we really ought to arrange something.

Judge What do you mean exactly?

Warden Well, you know . . .

Judge What, a bribe?

Warden Yes, a backhander, you know . . .

Judge No, too risky, dammit. He'll howl the place down, a Government man. Not unless we make a donation, say, from the local gentry, towards some monument or other.

Postmaster What if we say: 'Look, here's some money just arrived through the post, we've no idea who it belongs to'?

Warden Yes, well, you'd better watch he doesn't post *you*, to some far-off land! Listen, in a well-ordered society people don't do these things. And what are we all lined up here for, like a cavalry charge? We ought to present

ourselves to him one by one, so it's private, and, er . . .
to keep things right – so other people can't hear. That's
what happens in a well-ordered society. Right then,
Judge – you can go first.

Judge   No no – it's better if you go. After all, our
distinguished visitor did break bread in your hospital.

Warden   Actually, the Superintendent should go first,
as the torch-bearer to our youth.

Superintendent   No, I can't, sirs – I can't do it.
Perhaps it's my upbringing, but honestly, the minute
someone even one rank higher than me starts speaking,
my mind goes blank, and I get completely tongue-tied.
No, sirs, please, count me out!

Warden   Well, Judge, I suppose that leaves you. Go
on, you'd even be a match for Cicero.

Judge   Oh, rubbish! Cicero, really! Just because a man
gets carried away now and again, talking about his dogs,
or a fine bloodhound . . .

All (*urging him*)   No, no, Judge – not just dogs, you
could've talked up the Tower of Babel! Judge, please,
don't let us down, you're like a father to us! Please,
don't abandon us!

Judge   Gentlemen, leave me be!

Just then, footsteps and coughing are heard from **Khlestakov**'*s
room. They all make a mad rush to escape from the room,
bunching together, and some of them become wedged in the door.
Stifled cries of pain.*

Bobchinsky   Ouch! Dobchinsky, you're standing on
my foot!

Warden   Let me through, sirs, have a heart! You're
squeezing me to death!

*More cries of 'Ouch!', etc., until finally all manage to squeeze out,
leaving the room empty.* **Khlestakov** *then emerges, bleary-eyed.*

Khlestakov Well, I must've had a decent snooze. I
wonder where they got all those mattresses and
eiderdowns? I'm dripping with sweat. I think they
must've slipped me something at lunch yesterday – my
head's still thumping. Yes, from what I've seen, I could
pass the time very pleasantly here. I do enjoy hospitality,
and all the more so when it's out of the goodness of
people's hearts, and not some ulterior motive. The
Mayor's daughter's not bad-looking, and his wife'd do a
turn, too ... I don't know, I quite fancy this way of life.

The **Judge** *enters, and stops by the door.*

Judge (*aside*) Oh Lord, oh Lord! Help me out here,
please! My knees are giving way ... (*Aloud, drawing himself
up to his full height, his hand on his sword-hilt.*) Sir, permit
me to introduce myself – Collegiate Assessor, and
presiding Judge of the District Court – Lyapkin-Tyapkin.

Khlestakov Sit down, please. So – you're the law in
these parts?

Judge Yes, sir – appointed in 1816 for a three-year
term, at the instance of the local nobility, and continued
in that post until the present.

Khlestakov I see. And is it a profitable business,
being a judge?

Judge Well, sir, after three full terms of office I was
recommended for the Order of St Vladimir, Fourth
Class, with my superiors' approval. (*Aside.*) Oh Lord, this
money's burning a hole in my fist!

Khlestakov Oh, I do like the Vladimir. It leaves the
St Anne Third Class simply nowhere.

Judge (*slowly extending his clenched fist. Aside*) God
almighty – I feel as if I'm sitting on hot coals!

Khlestakov What's that you have in your hand?

Judge (*panics, and drops the banknotes on the floor*) Nothing,
sir!

Khlestakov   What d'you mean nothing? Didn't I see money falling?

Judge (*trembling all over*)   No no, it was absolutely nothing, sir! (*Aside.*) Oh Lord, I'm in the dock now! And the cart's arrived to whisk me off to jail!

Khlestakov (*picking it up*)   Yes, it is money.

Judge (*aside*)   The game's up! I'm done for!

Khlestakov   Look, I'll tell you what – why don't you give me a loan of this?

Judge (*eagerly*)   Oh yes, sir, yes! With the greatest of pleasure! (*Aside.*) Now, go to it! Holy Mother of God, see me through this!

Khlestakov   I ran out of cash on the road, you see, what with one thing and another . . . Anyway, I'll send it back to you from my estate.

Judge   Oh, please, don't even mention it – I'm only too honoured. Naturally, I endeavour to serve my superiors to the utmost of my abilities, meagre though they be . . . (*Rises from his chair and comes to attention.*) Sir, I shall not presume to trouble you further with my presence. Does Your Honour have any instructions for me?

Khlestakov   What sort of instructions?

Judge   Well, I thought you might perhaps have some instructions for the District Court?

Khlestakov   What on earth for? I've no business in that place now, surely?

Judge (*bows and makes to exit. Aside*)   Yes, we've won the day!

Khlestakov (*after he has gone*)   Decent chap, the Judge.

Enter the **Postmaster**, *stiffly, his hand on his sword-hilt.*

Postmaster Sir, permit me to introduce myself –
Postmaster and Court Councillor Shpyokin.

Khlestakov Ah, I'm delighted to meet you. I do
enjoy good company. Please, sit down. So, you've always
lived here?

Postmaster That's correct, Your Honour.

Khlestakov Yes, I rather like this little town. Not
many people, of course, but so what? It's not the capital.
It's not exactly St Petersburg, is it?

Postmaster That's perfectly true, sir.

Khlestakov Yes, the capital's your only place for *le
bon ton* – none of your provincial clods there, eh? What's
your opinion?

Postmaster That's absolutely right, sir. (*Aside.*) Well,
one thing – he isn't too proud to ask questions.

Khlestakov Even so, you can live quite contentedly in
a small town, wouldn't you say?

Postmaster Yes, indeed, sir.

Khlestakov You know what I think? I think all you
need is a bit of respect, a bit of sincere affection, *n'est-ce
pas*?

Postmaster I couldn't agree more, sir.

Khlestakov You know, I'm really pleased we're of the
same mind. Of course, people will say I'm a queer fish,
but that's just how I am. (*Peers closely at him, then aside.*) I
think I'll tap this Postmaster for a loan! (*Aloud.*) You
know, it's the damndest thing: I absolutely ran out of
cash on the road. I don't suppose you could see your
way to lending me three hundred roubles?

Postmaster Yes, why not? With the greatest of
pleasure, sir. Here, take it, please. I'm delighted to be of
service.

Khlestakov Thank you very much. I must confess, I positively loathe having to do without things when I'm travelling, and why on earth should I? D'you agree?

Postmaster Oh, completely, sir. (*Stands up, and comes to attention, his hand on his sword-hilt.*) Sir, I shall not presume to trouble you further with my presence. Does Your Honour wish to make any observations pertaining to the postal administration?

Khlestakov No, none at all.

The **Postmaster** *bows and exits.*

Khlestakov The Postmaster seems a decent chap too. Obliging, at any rate. My sort of people.

Enter the **Superintendent**, *virtually shoved through the door. A voice is almost audible behind him: 'What are you scared of?' The* **Superintendent** *comes to attention, hand on sword-hilt, in a state of some trepidation.*

Superintendent Sir, permit me to introduce myself – Superintendent of Schools and Titular Councillor Khlopov.

Khlestakov Pleased to meet you! Sit down, sit down. Would you care for a cigar? (*Offers him a cigar.*)

Superintendent (*aside, indecisive*) Oh Lord, what now! I never expected this. Should I take it or shouldn't I?

Khlestakov Go on, take it, man. It's not a bad smoke. Not up to Petersburg standard, of course. No, old chap, I used to pay twenty-five roubles a hundred, really fine cigars – my God, you'd feel like kissing your hands after you'd smoked one. Here, light up. (*Hands him a candle.*)

The **Superintendent** *tries to light the cigar, trembling all over.*

Khlestakov   No, that's the wrong end, man!

The **Superintendent** *drops the cigar out of sheer fright, spits, and flaps his arms.*

Superintendent (*aside*)   Damn these nerves of mine! They'll ruin everything!

Khlestakov   Well, I can see you're not a cigar hand. I must admit they're one of my weaknesses. That and the fair sex, of course – I can't say I'm indifferent to them. What about you? Which do you prefer – blondes or brunettes?

The **Superintendent** *is completely at a loss.*

Khlestakov   Come on, man, out with it – blondes or brunettes?

Superintendent   I wouldn't presume to know, sir.

Khlestakov   Come on, you're not going to weasel out of it. I absolutely insist on knowing your preference.

Superintendent   Well, sir, if I might venture an opinion . . . (*Aside.*) Oh Lord, I don't know *what* to say!

Khlestakov   Aha! You won't tell, eh? Why, I'll wager some little brunette's got her claws into you. She has, hasn't she – come on, admit it!

The **Superintendent** *is silent.*

Khlestakov   Ho-ho! You're blushing! You see? You see? Why won't you tell me?

Superintendent   Your Hon . . . Your Gra . . . Your High . . . Oh, I'm too afraid! (*Aside.*) This damn tongue's let me down again!

Khlestakov   Afraid? Yes, I suppose there is something in my eyes that makes people go a bit weak at the knees. Certainly I know the ladies can't resist them, am I right?

Superintendent   Oh, absolutely correct, sir.

Khlestakov   Well, anyway, it's the damndest thing, but would you believe, I got completely wiped out on the road. You couldn't lend me three hundred roubles, I suppose?

Superintendent (*groping in his pockets, aside*)   Oh Lord, what if I haven't got it! Yes, yes, it's here! (*Pulls out some banknotes and hands them over, trembling.*)

Khlestakov   Thank you very much.

Superintendent (*comes to attention, hand on sword-hilt*) Sir, I shall not presume to trouble you further with my presence.

Khlestakov   Goodbye!

Superintendent (*practically flies out of the room. Aside*) Thank God for that! With any luck he won't even look at the school.

Enter the **Charities Warden**, *who comes to attention, hand on sword-hilt.*

Warden   Sir, permit me to introduce myself: Warden of Charitable Institutions, Court Councillor Zemlyanika.

Khlestakov   Good morning. Do sit down, please.

Warden   I had the honour to receive you in person, sir, and accompany you on your inspection of those institutions entrusted to my care.

Khlestakov   Oh yes, I remember now. You did us a very decent lunch.

Warden   I am only too pleased to be of service to my country.

Khlestakov   Yes, I must confess that's one of my weaknesses – I do like good food. Actually, I had the impression you were a little bit shorter yesterday – was I right?

Warden Quite possibly, sir. (*After a pause.*) I can truthfully say I never spare myself in the execution of my duties. (*Draws his chair a little closer and speaks in a half-whisper.*) Actually, the Postmaster here does absolutely nothing. The whole business is in an advanced state of neglect, parcels get held up . . . you might well investigate that. The Judge too, who was in here just before me, spends all his time hare-coursing, and keeps his hounds in the court-house, and as for his conduct – I feel obliged to say this, of course, only for the good of my country, although he's my own kith and kin, and a friend – well, his conduct is utterly reprehensible. There's a certain landowner here, Dobchinsky – I believe you've met him, sir – well, no sooner does Dobchinsky step out of the house, than the Judge is sitting there with his wife. And I'm ready to swear to that, sir – you just take a look at the children: not one of them looks like Dobchinsky, they're all the spitting image of the Judge, even the little girl!

Khlestakov You don't say! I'd never have believed it.

Warden And then there's our Superintendent of Schools . . . I don't know how the authorities could have entrusted him with such a position. He's worse than a French revolutionary, he fills our young people's heads with such pernicious ideas that I hardly dare utter them aloud. Perhaps you'd like me to put all this down on paper?

Khlestakov Yes, on paper, by all means. That'll be splendid. I really enjoy having something amusing to read when I'm bored. By the way, what's your name? I keep forgetting.

Warden It's Zemlyanika, sir.

Khlestakov Ah yes, Zemlyanika. And tell me, do you have any children?

Warden Indeed I have, sir – five. Two of them

already grown up.

Khlestakov   Grown up, fancy that! So what are they
. . . er, what are their. . . ?

Warden   I take it Your Honour is enquiring as to
their names?

Khlestakov   Yes, what are they called?

Warden   Nikolai, Ivan, Yelizaveta, Marya, and
Perepetuya.

Khlestakov   That's nice.

Warden   Sir, I shall not presume to trouble you
further with my presence, taking up time which I'm sure
you have allotted to your sacred duties . . . (*Bows and
makes to leave.*)

Khlestakov (*accompanying him to the door*)   Think nothing
of it. It's all very amusing, what you've been saying. Do
please come again. I've enjoyed this hugely. (*Turns back
and opens the door, calls after him.*) Wait, hold on! Who did
you say you were? I keep forgetting your name.

Warden   It's Zemlyanika, sir. Artemy Filipovich.

Khlestakov   Well, look, Artemy old chap, it's the
damndest thing, but I got cleaned out completely on the
road. You haven't any money you could lend me – say,
four hundred roubles?

Warden   I have, sir.

Khlestakov   Really? That's very handy. Thank you so
much.

The **Warden** *hands over the money and exits. Enter*
Bobchinsky *and* **Dobchinsky**.

Bobchinsky   Sir, permit me to introduce myself: Pyotr
Ivanovich Bobchinsky, resident of this town.

Dobchinsky   And Pyotr Ivanovich Dobchinsky,
landowner.

Khlestakov (*to* **Bobchinsky**)   Ah yes, I've seen you before. You fell over, I think. So, how's the nose?

Bobchinsky   Oh, don't concern yourself, sir. It's healed up now, thank goodness, dry as a bone.

Khlestakov   Good, I'm glad to hear it. Yes, delighted . . . (*Abruptly.*) Got any money on you?

Bobchinsky   Money? What for?

Khlestakov (*rapidly*)   For a loan of a thousand roubles.

Bobchinsky   Good heavens, I don't have that kind of money. What about you, Dobchinsky?

Dobchinsky   No, sir, nor do I, to be honest. All my money's lodged with the Board of Guardians, doing good works, you see.

Khlestakov   Well, if you can't run to a thousand, make it a hundred.

Bobchinsky (*rummaging in his pockets*)   Dobchinsky, you haven't got a hundred roubles, have you? All I've got is forty in notes.

Dobchinsky (*looks in his wallet*)   Twenty-five, and that's the lot.

Bobchinsky   Have another look, Dobchinsky, for heaven's sake! You've got a hole in your right-hand pocket, I know you have. It's probably slipped through.

Dobchinsky   No, there's nothing there, honestly.

Khlestakov   Well, no matter. I'll get by. You can let me have the sixty-five roubles, that'll be fine. (*Takes the money.*)

Dobchinsky   Sir, if I might make so bold as to ask your assistance on a rather delicate matter . . .

Khlestakov   Yes, what is it?

Dobchinsky   Really, it's an extremely delicate business: you see, my eldest boy, Your Honour, was born out of wedlock.

Khlestakov   Indeed?

Dobchinsky   Well, in a manner of speaking, that is – he was born just the same as if it were in wedlock, and I put everything to rights afterwards, Your Honour, within the bonds of matrimony, so to speak. Anyway, if you could see your way clear, Your Honour – what I'd like now is for him to be my son and heir – legitimate, I mean – and take my name – Dobchinsky.

Khlestakov   Fine, let him take it. No problem.

Dobchinsky   I wouldn't have troubled Your Honour, but it's a real shame, on account of his abilities. He's a remarkable lad, shows great promise: he can recite all sorts of poems by heart, and he's only got to pick up a penknife, and he'll carve you a tiny little droshky quick as a flash. Bobchinsky'll tell you.

Bobchinsky   Yes, he's a talented lad.

Khlestakov   Good, good! I'll see what I can do, I'll have a word with . . . I'm sure I can . . . oh, I'll sort something out, yes, of course. (*Turns to* **Bobchinsky**.) And what about you? Have you nothing for me?

Bobchinsky   Well, sir, when you go back to Petersburg, I'd be most deeply grateful if you'd just say to all those bigwigs there, all those senators and admirals: 'Look, Your Highness, or Your Excellency or whatever, there's this town, and there's a chap called Bobchinsky living there . . .' Just say: 'There's a chap called Bobchinsky.'

Khlestakov   Fine, I'll do that.

Bobchinsky   And if you should happen to run into the Emperor, then tell him too. Say: 'You know, Your Imperial Majesty, there's a certain town, and there's a chap called Bobchinsky.'

Khlestakov Fine, I'll do that.

Dobchinsky Sir, I do apologise for burdening you
with my presence.

Bobchinsky Sir, I do apologise for burdening you
with my presence.

Khlestakov Not at all. It's been my pleasure. (*Shows
them out, then to himself.*) Well, there's a lot of civil servants
in this place. I think they must've mistaken me for some
high Government official. True enough, I did put on the
dog a bit yesterday. What imbeciles! I must drop a note
to Tryapichkin in Petersburg about this. He writes all
those articles – he'll make mincemeat out of this lot.
Hey, Osip, fetch me some paper and ink!

Osip *pops his head round the door, says: 'Right sir!'*

Khlestakov By God, once Tryapichkin gets his teeth
into you – watch out! He wouldn't even spare his own
father, if there was a joke in it, and he's not averse to
cash, either. Actually, these people are quite decent.
After all, they have been lending me money, that's a
point in their favour, surely. I'd better check, see how
much I've got. Now, that's three hundred from the
Judge, three hundred from the Postmaster – that makes
six hundred ... seven hundred ... eight hundred ...
ugh, what a greasy note! ... eight hundred ... nine
hundred ... ho-ho! That's over a thousand! By God,
just let that infantry captain turn up now. We'll see who
gets skinned this time!

Enter **Osip** *with ink and paper.*

Khlestakov Now, you oaf, you see? You see how well
I'm looked after? (*Begins writing.*)

Osip I do, thanks be to God. But I'll tell you
something, master.

Khlestakov   Oh, and what's that?

Osip   You want to clear off out of here. While the going's good, believe me.

Khlestakov   Oh, rubbish! What for?

Osip   Because. Just cut and run, sir. We've had a right good couple of days here, and that'll do us. You don't want any more dealings with these people – to hell with 'em! It'd be just our luck if somebody was to turn up. Honest to God, master! And they've got some dandy horses, we'd be out of here in no time.

Khlestakov (*writing*)   No, I think I'll hang around a bit longer. Maybe tomorrow.

Osip   What d'you mean tomorrow? Master, let's go now, for God's sake! All right, so they're treating you like royalty, but the sooner we make tracks the better. It's obvious they've mistaken you for somebody else. And your father'll be spitting mad if we don't get a move on. We could roll out of here in style – they'd give us top-class horses.

Khlestakov   Oh, all right then. Just take this letter first, and you might as well order the post-horses while you're at it. And make sure they're the best! Tell the coachmen I'll give them a rouble apiece, to drive me like one of His Majesty's couriers, and sing songs on the way! (*Continues writing.*) Tryapichkin'll die laughing, I can just imagine . . .

Osip   Sir, I'll send one of the men here with this, I'll get busy with the packing, so we don't waste any time.

Khlestakov (*writing*)   Fine, fine – just bring me a candle.

Osip (*exits and speaks off-stage*)   Hey, you – listen! You've to take a letter to the post office, and tell the Postmaster he's not to charge for it. Yes, and tell him to send round his best troika – same as he keeps for the couriers

– and the gentleman's not paying the hire on that neither. It's official business, tell him. Now come on, look lively, afore his lordship loses his temper. Wait, wait – the letter's not finished yet.

Khlestakov (*continuing to write*)   I wonder where he's staying these days – Post Office Street or Gorokhovaya? He's another one for changing his lodgings, and not paying his rent. Well, I'll address it to Post Office Street on the off-chance. (*Folds the letter and addresses it.*)

Osip *brings the candle, and* **Khlestakov** *seals up the letter. Just then, Constable* **Derzhimorda** *is heard outside: 'Hey, you with the beard – where d'you think you're going? Nobody's allowed in here, that's orders.'* **Khlestakov** *hands* **Osip** *the letter.*

Khlestakov   Right, take it away.

Shopkeepers (*off-stage*)   Let us through, sir. You can't keep us out. We're here on business.

Derzhimorda (*off-stage*)   Clear off! Come on, break it up! He's not seeing anybody, he's asleep.

The hubbub increases.

Khlestakov   What's going on out there, Osip? See what that noise is.

Osip (*looks out of the window*)   It's shopkeepers, sir, and the like – they're trying to come in but the constable won't let 'em. They're waving bits of paper: I think they want to see you.

Khlestakov (*goes over to the window*)   Yes, what is it you want, dear friends?

Shopkeepers (*off-stage*)   Your Honour, we've come to beg a favour. Tell them to let us in, sir – receive our petitions.

Khlestakov   Let these men in, d'you hear! Let them in. Osip, tell them to come in.

Osip *exits.* **Khlestakov** *accepts the petitions through the window, opens one and begins reading it.*

Khlestakov 'From the merchant Abdulin, to His Most Serene Magnificence, the Lord High Financier . . .' What the devil's this? There's no such personage.

The **Shopkeepers** *enter, carrying a basket of wine and sugar-loaves.*

Khlestakov Now, what can I do for you, my dear sirs?

Shopkeepers Your Honour, we most humbly crave your indulgence!

Khlestakov What is it you want?

Shopkeepers Save us from ruin, sir! We're being shamefully abused, for no reason.

Khlestakov By whom?

A Shopkeeper It's all because of the Mayor here, sir. There's never been a mayor like him, Your Honour. The things he gets away with, you wouldn't believe. He billets soldiers in our homes, sir – honestly, you might as well put your head in a noose. He just doesn't know when to stop. He'll grab you by the beard and shout: 'Come on, you heathen!' Honest to God, sir! I mean, if we'd been disrespectful, fair enough, but we've always done right by him: a bit of dress material for his wife and daughter – we don't mind that at all. But oh no, that's not enough for him. No, he just walks into the shop and takes whatever he fancies. He'll see a bolt of cloth, he'll say: 'You've some nice stuff there, my good man – send that round to me, will you?' So you've got to take it round, and there's all of fifty yards in that piece.

Khlestakov Really? Why, the man's a scoundrel!

Shopkeepers Honest to God, sir! Nobody can

remember a mayor like him. You have to hide
everything in the shop, the minute you see him coming.
And he's not fussy, either, he'll take any old rubbish:
prunes, say, that've been lying in the barrel for seven
years, that even my message-boy wouldn't touch, and
he'll eat them by the fistful! His name-day falls on St
Anton's, and of course, you shower him with presents,
you'd think he lacked for nothing, but no, you've got to
do the same again – he says his name-day's St Hilarios
as well! And what can you do, except give him more
presents?

Khlestakov   Highway robbery!

Shopkeepers   Too true! And if you dare say a word
against him, he'll billet a whole regiment on you. Either
that or he'll close you down. 'I can't order corporal
punishment,' he'll tell you, 'or have you tortured,
because that's against the law, but by God,' he'll say,
'you'll be on bread and water, if it's up to me!'

Khlestakov   Conniving wretch, he should go straight
to Siberia!

Shopkeepers   Or anywhere Your Honour cares to
send him, that's fine by us, as long as it's far away.
Now, good sir, please don't turn down our hospitality –
see, we've brought you a little hamper of wine, and
some sugar-loaves.

Khlestakov   Heavens no, don't even think of it: I
don't accept any sort of bribes. On the other hand, if
you were to offer me a loan, say, of three hundred
roubles – well, that's a different matter. Loans I can
accept.

Shopkeepers   Oh, please do. Your Honour! (*Fishing
out money.*) And why only three hundred? Take five
hundred, better still – just help us, please!

Khlestakov   Well, I won't say no – but it's a loan,
mind.

Shopkeepers (*presenting him with the money on a silver tray*)   Here you are, Your Honour, and please, keep the tray.

Khlestakov   Mm, I suppose I can.

Shopkeepers (*bowing*)   And take the sugar-loaves along with it.

Khlestakov   No no, I don't accept bribes.

Osip   Oh, go on, take it, Your Magnificence – why not? Take it! It'll come in handy on the road. Look, give me the sugar, and the bag. I'll take the lot, it won't go to waste. What's that, string? Give me that as well – you can always find a use for a bit of string, like say, if the wagon comes apart or something, you can tie it up.

Shopkeepers   So you'll look kindly on our petition, Your Excellency? Truly, if you can't help us, we don't know what we'll do – stick our heads in a noose, most like.

Khlestakov   Oh, for sure, absolutely. I'll do my level best.

The **Shopkeepers** *exit. A woman's voice is heard off-stage: 'Don't you dare keep me out! I'll complain to His Honour about you too! Ow! Don't push, you're hurting me!'*

Khlestakov   Who's that? (*Crosses to the window.*) What's the matter, woman?

Two Women (*off-stage*)   Have mercy on us, Your Honour, please! Tell 'em to let us in, sir – give us a hearing!

Khlestakov (*through the window*)   Let them in.

Enter the **Locksmith's wife** *and the* **Sergeant's widow**.

Locksmith's wife (*bowing deeply*)   Oh, sir, I beg you . . .

Sergeant's widow   Have mercy on us!

Khlestakov Who are you, good women?

Sergeant's widow Sir, I'm Sergeant Ivanov's widow.

Locksmith's wife And I'm a local woman, Your Honour – Fevronya Poshlyopkin, the locksmith's wife.

Khlestakov Hold on, one at a time, please. What is it you want?

Locksmith's wife Have mercy on me, sir: I want to complain about the Mayor, God rot him! May he rot in hell, sir, him and his brats and his whole tribe, aunts and uncles and all – I hope they get no good out of nothing, not ever!

Khlestakov Heavens, why not?

Locksmith's wife 'Cause he had my husband called up into the army, sir, the thieving swine, and it weren't his turn, neither. He's a married man, Your Honour, it ain't legal.

Khlestakov How'd he manage that, for God's sake?

Locksmith's wife Oh, he managed, sir, the scheming rat – may God strike him down, in this world and the next, yes! I hope he meets a bad end, sir, him and his aunt, if he's got one, yes, and his father, if he's still alive – I hope he snuffs it too, the miserable old crow, I hope he chokes on his porridge! He was supposed to send the tailor's boy, he's a drunken pig anyway, but his folks've got money, they bought him off, so then he picks on old Panteleeva's son, her that keeps the shop, and Panteleeva sends the Mayor's wife three bolts of cloth, so he's onto me next. 'What d'you need a husband for anyway?' he says. 'He's no use to you.' Well, whether he's any use or not, I says, that's my business, you conniving old villain! 'He's a thief,' he says. 'And if he hasn't stolen anything yet, he soon enough will, and he'll be conscripted next year anyway, so what's the odds?' And what am I supposed to do with no husband, I says,

you rotten crook? I'm a poor weak woman, you
miserable wretch! By God, I hope none of your family
ever sees the light of day again! And if you've got a
mother-in-law, I hope she . . .

Khlestakov   Yes, yes, I get the gist. Well, then – and
what about you? (*Showing the* **Locksmith's wife** *out.*)

Locksmith's wife   Don't forget, please. Your Honour!
Have mercy on us!

Sergeant's widow   Sir, I've come about the Mayor
too . . .

Khlestakov   Well, get on with it then – and keep it
short.

Sergeant's widow   He had me flogged, Your
Honour!

Khlestakov   What?

Sergeant's widow   It was all a mistake, sir. Some of
us women was having a bit of a set-to at the market,
and the police didn't turn up in time, so they just
grabbed me for it. Beat the living daylights out of me,
they did – I couldn't sit down for a week.

Khlestakov   So what can I do about it now?

Sergeant's widow   There's not much you can do, sir,
of course, but you can order him to pay me
compensation for the mistake. I could do with a spot of
luck right now, and the money would come in handy.

Khlestakov   All right, fine. Now run along, and I'll
see what I can do.

Various hands are thrusting petitions in through the window.

Who's this next? (*Crosses to the window.*) No, I don't want
these! Take them away! (*Withdraws.*) Oh, to hell with
this, I've had enough! Osip, don't let them in!

Osip (*shouts through the window*)   Go away! Go on, clear off! Time's up, come back tomorrow!

The door opens to reveal a figure in a shoddy greatcoat, unshaven, with a swollen lip and a bandaged jaw. Several others can be seen in the background behind him.

Osip   Clear off, I said! Where d'you think you're going?

He gives the first man a shove in the stomach, and follows him out into the hall, slamming the door shut after him, and leaving **Khlestakov** *alone on stage. Enter the Mayor's daughter,* **Marya**.

Marya   Oh!

Khlestakov   Did I frighten you, dear lady?

Marya   No, I'm not frightened.

Khlestakov (*striking a pose*)   I must say I'm rather pleased at being taken for the sort of man who . . . May I presume to ask where you were intending to go?

Marya   Honestly, I wasn't going anywhere.

Khlestakov   And why, indeed, weren't you going anywhere?

Marya   I was just wondering if Mama was here.

Khlestakov   No no, I really would like to know *why* you weren't going anywhere.

Marya   Sir, I've disturbed you. You have important business to attend to.

Khlestakov (*striking another pose*)   But aren't your lovely eyes more important than my business? There's no way you could disturb me, none whatsoever. On the contrary, you can afford me nothing but pleasure.

Marya   Oh, you speak so beautifully – just like they do in Petersburg!

Khlestakov   To so beautiful a creature as yourself,

yes. May I make so bold as to offer you a chair? I
should be so happy. Heavens, no – not a chair – for
you, it should be a throne!

Marya Really, I don't know ... I ought to be going,
honestly. (*Sits.*)

Khlestakov What an exquisite scarf you're wearing!

Marya You're making fun of me – you like having a
laugh at us provincials.

Khlestakov Oh, dear lady, how I long to be that
scarf of yours, to embrace your lily-white neck.

Marya I can't imagine what you mean. It's just an
old scarf – 'cause the weather's a bit up and down
today.

Khlestakov My dear lady, what matter any kind of
weather, beside your beautiful lips!

Marya Gracious, the things you say! I wouldn't mind
asking you to write something in my album – some
verse, for a keepsake. I bet you know lots of poems.

Khlestakov For you, sweet lady – anything, anything.
What sort of verses would you like?

Marya Oh, any sort, I don't mind. Something nice
and new.

Khlestakov Ah yes, verses, verses! I know heaps.

Marya Tell me what you're going to write – say
them.

Khlestakov What's the point of reciting them? I know
them well enough.

Marya I do so love poetry.

Khlestakov You see, I know so many – all sorts of
poems. Oh, all right – what about this, then?

'*O, man, that in thy sorrows dost cry out*

In vain upon the Lord thy God!

There's others besides, I just can't call them to mind. Anyway, that's neither here nor there. I'd much rather declare my love – the love I feel, gazing into your eyes . . . (*Moves his chair closer.*)

Marya Love! I don't understand love. I've never even known what it was. (*Moves her chair away.*)

Khlestakov (*moving closer*) Why are you pulling your chair away? We'll be much cosier sitting close together.

Marya (*moving away*) Why sit closer? Why not further away?

Khlestakov (*moving closer*) What d'you mean further away? Why not closer?

Marya (*moving away*) What on earth are you up to?

Khlestakov (*moving closer*) Believe me, you only imagine we're close together, so just imagine we're far apart instead. Oh, my dear lady, how happy I'd be if I could enfold you in my arms, and press you to my bosom!

Marya (*looks out of the window*) Oh look, I'm sure that was a bird that just flew past. Was it a magpie, d'you think, or some other sort?

Khlestakov (*kisses her shoulder, and looks out of the window*) It was a magpie.

Marya (*springs up in indignation*) Oh, this is going too far! What a cheek!

Khlestakov (*trying to restrain her*) Forgive me, dear lady! It was love that made me do it, nothing but love!

Marya Obviously you take me for some country wench, the sort who . . .

Khlestakov (*still trying to restrain her*) It was love, I swear, simple affection. An innocent bit of fun, dearest lady, please don't be angry. I'll go down on my knees and beg your forgiveness! (*Kneels.*) Forgive me, please, please. Look, I'm on my knees to you.

Enter the Mayor's wife, **Anna**.

Anna (*seeing* **Khlestakov** *on his knees*) Oh! What a scene!

Khlestakov (*rising*) Damn!

Anna (*to her daughter*) What's the meaning of this, young lady? What sort of behaviour do you call this?

Marya Mama, dearest, I . . .

Anna Get out of my sight! Get out, d'you hear! And don't dare show your face in here again! (**Marya** *exits in tears.*) You'll forgive me, sir, but I must confess I'm quite taken aback . . .

Khlestakov (*aside*) She's quite appetising herself – not bad at all. (*Drops to his knees again.*) Oh, dear lady, you see how I'm consumed with love!

Anna What are you doing on your knees? Stand up, stand up, for goodness' sake! I mean, the floor's not even clean.

Khlestakov No, no, I must kneel, I absolutely must! I must know my fate – whether life, or death!

Anna I'm sorry, sir, but I'm not sure I fully understand you. If I'm not mistaken, you're making a declaration of love for my daughter.

Khlestakov No, no, it's you I'm in love with, ma'am – you! My life hangs by a thread. If you won't requite my undying love, then I am unworthy to walk this earth. I ask for your hand, with a fierce flame of love burning in my breast!

Anna Sir, if you'll permit me to observe, I am, in a manner of speaking – a married woman.

Khlestakov   Who cares! True love knows no such distinctions. As the great Karamzin himself says: ''Tis but man's law condemns!' Madame, let us withdraw to some shady rill ... your hand, I implore you, give me your hand!

Marya *suddenly rushes into the room.*

Marya   Mama, Papa says you've got to ... (*Seeing* **Khlestakov** *on his knees, lets out a shriek.*) Oh! What a scene!

Anna   What's the matter with you? What are you on about? Eh? Lord, what a silly creature! Running in here like a scalded cat – what are you standing there goggling at? What on earth's going on in that head of yours? Honestly, she's like a three-year-old infant. You'd never believe it – never in a month of Sundays would you believe she was eighteen years old! Heaven only knows when you're going to get some sense, and start behaving like a decent, well brought-up young woman! There are rules, you know, of good conduct and decorum – just when are you going to learn them?

Marya (*in tears*)   Mama, I had no idea ...

Anna   No, of course you hadn't – you've got nothing but air between your ears, that's why! You take your example from those Lyapkin-Tyapkin girls, the Judge's daughters. I don't know why you even look at them. Why copy them, for heaven's sake? It's not as if you've no better examples – your own mother, for a start, right here looking at you. That's the sort of example you should follow.

Khlestakov (*seizing* **Marya**'s *hand*)   Anna Andreevna, please don't stand in the way of our happiness. Give your blessing to our undying love!

Anna (*bewildered*)   What? So *she's* the one ... ?

Khlestakov   Make your decision: life, or death!

Anna Well now, you see, you silly creature? You see what you've done? Because of you, all that stupid nonsense of yours, our guest has to go down on his knees, and you come rushing in like a mad thing. Honestly, I ought to refuse my consent. You just don't deserve such happiness.

Marya Oh, Mama, I won't do it again. Truly I won't.

Enter the **Mayor**, *out of breath.*

Mayor Oh, Your Excellency! Please don't ruin us! Don't destroy us, please!

Khlestakov What on earth's the matter?

Mayor It's those shopkeepers – sir – they've been complaining to Your Excellency. I swear to you on my honour, sir, you can't believe the half of what they say! They're the biggests cheats going, sir, them and their short weight. And the sergeant's widow, the one I'm supposed to have flogged – she's lying in her teeth, I swear to God. She flogged herself – yes, she did!

Khlestakov Oh, the hell with your sergeant's widow – what's she got to do with me?

Mayor Don't believe a word of it, Your Honour! They're such damnable liars, sir – a babe in arms could see through them! They're famous for their lies, sir, the whole town knows them. And when it comes to swindling, well, if I may make so bold, Your Honour, you'll not find their equal on land or sea!

Anna Anton, you surely can't be aware of the honour His Excellency is bestowing upon us. He's asking for our daughter's hand in marriage.

Mayor What! What! Good God, woman, have you gone mad! Oh, Your Excellency, please don't be angry. She's not right in the head, her mother was just the same.

Khlestakov   No, it's true – I am asking for her hand. I'm in love.

Mayor   Your Excellency ... I can't believe it.

Anna   For heaven's sake, he's telling you!

Khlestakov   I'm not joking, sir. I'm ready to run mad with love.

Mayor   No no, I daren't believe it, I'm not worthy of such an honour.

Khlestakov   Sir, if you don't consent to give me your daughter's hand, God only knows what I'll do!

Mayor   I can't believe it. You're pulling my leg, surely, Your Excellency.

Anna   Oh, you great stupid oaf! Why can't you get it into your thick head?

Mayor   I just can't believe it.

Khlestakov   Your consent, for God's sake! I'm a desperate man, sir, I'm capable of anything. And when I shoot myself, it'll be your neck!

Mayor   Oh, my God, please, no! I'm innocent, I swear, body and soul! Don't be angry, sir, please. Do whatever Your Honour sees fit, I beg you. To tell you the truth, my head's in an absolute ... I haven't a clue what's going on. I've made a complete idiot of myself, the biggest idiot that ever was.

Anna   Well, go on, give them your blessing!

Khlestakov *steps forward with* **Marya**.

Mayor   God bless you both. I'm innocent, I tell you!

Khlestakov *kisses* **Marya**, *while the* **Mayor** *looks on*.

Mayor   What the devil! It is, it's true! (*Rubbing his eyes.*) They're actually kissing! Oh, my God, they're kissing! They're engaged! (*Shouts and jumps for joy.*) Oh, Anton,

Anton! Yes, Your Worship! Yes, Mister Mayor! Now, there's a turn up!

Osip *enters.*

Osip Sir, that's the horses ready.

Khlestakov Fine, I'll be down in a minute.

Mayor What's that, sir? You're not leaving?

Khlestakov Yes, I have to go.

Mayor But when, Your Honour? I mean, it was you yourself, sir, that was hinting about a wedding . . .

Khlestakov Oh yes, that . . . Look, I only need a minute . . . just a day or so to see my uncle – he's a wealthy old stick – and I'll be back without fail tomorrow.

Mayor Oh well, we wouldn't dream of detaining you, sir, and we'll look forward to Your Honour's safe return.

Khlestakov Yes, yes, of course – I'll be straight back. *Au revoir, mon amour!* No, no, I simply can't express what I feel! Goodbye, my darling! (*Kisses her hand.*)

Mayor Are you sure you don't need anything for the road, Your Honour? I believe you were a little short of cash?

Khlestakov Heavens no, where'd you get that idea? (*Thinks a moment.*) Well, possibly.

Mayor How much would you like?

Khlestakov Well, that two hundred you loaned me – or four hundred, I should say, I don't want to take advantage of your mistake – perhaps you could let me have the same again, make it a round eight hundred.

Mayor With pleasure! (*Takes the money out of his wallet.*) There you are, crisp new notes too, for the occasion.

Khlestakov Oh, yes. (*Accepts the notes and inspects them.*)

These'll do nicely. Don't they say new notes bring you luck?

Mayor   They do indeed, sir.

Khlestakov   Well, goodbye, my dear friend. I'm much obliged to you for your hospitality. Yes, I must say in all sincerity, sir, I've never received such a warm welcome. (*To* **Anna**.) Goodbye, dear lady! (*To* **Marya**.) Goodbye, my darling!

All exit. For the remainder of the scene, their voices are heard off-stage.

Khlestakov   Farewell, my angel, dearest Marya!

Mayor   Good gracious, sir, you're surely not travelling in a post-chaise? They're so uncomfortable.

Khlestakov   Oh, I'm used to that. I get a headache in a sprung carriage.

Coachman   Whoa, there!

Mayor   Well, at the very least take something to spread on the seat, even just a rug. Shouldn't I order them to fetch Your Honour a rug?

Khlestakov   No, it's not worth bothering about. Oh well, I suppose a rug wouldn't come amiss.

Mayor   Hey, Avdotya! Go into the store-room and bring out the best rug – the one with the blue background, the Persian. And look lively!

Coachman   Whoa, there!

Mayor   So when may we expect Your Honour?

Khlestakov   Oh, tomorrow or the next day.

Osip   Is that the rug? Right, let's have it – put it down there. Now let's have a bit of hay round that side.

Coachman   Whoa, there!

Osip No, round this side! Here! A bit more. Right, that's fine. That'll do nicely. (*Pats the rug smooth.*) You can sit down now, Your Eminence.

Khlestakov Goodbye, my dear sir!

Mayor Goodbye, Your Excellency!

Khlestakov *Au revoir, chère maman!*

Coachman Giddy up, my lovelies!

Harness bells ring as they drive off. Curtain.

Act Five

The same room. The **Mayor**, *his wife* **Anna**, *and daughter* **Marya**.

Mayor Well, Anna my dear, what d'you think? Never imagined anything like that, eh? Dammit, what a prize catch! Come on, admit it – you'd never in your wildest dreams . . . a simple town-mayor's wife, and suddenly . . . Damn me, to find yourself related to a young devil like that!

Anna Oh, nothing of the sort. I could see it coming ages ago. Of course it's all marvellous to you, because you're just a peasant, you've never mixed with decent people.

Mayor Now then, Mother – I'm pretty decent myself. Anyway, just think, Anna, we're birds of a different feather now. What d'you think? By God, we're flying high all right! Just wait, I'll give it hot to all those whingers with their complaints and petitions. Hey! Who's out there? (*Enter the* **Constable**.) Ah, it's you, Svistunov. Fetch all those shopkeepers in here. By God, I'll sort them out, the rabble – complain about me, would they? Well, you wait, you damned Judases! Yes, you just wait, my darlings! I've given you a hiding before now, but this time I'll pulverise you! Make a note of their names, everybody that came here whining about me, and those wretched scribblers, especially, the ones that wrote out their complaints for them. Yes, and make an announcement, let them all know what a great honour God has bestowed on their Mayor – that he's marrying his daughter not to some peasant, but a person the like of which there's never been, a man who can do anything, absolutely anything! Announce it publicly, so they'll all get the message. Shout it in the streets, ring the bells till they crack, damn it! My God, if this isn't worth celebrating, then what is! (*The* **Constable** *exits*.)

Well now, Anna my dear, what d'you think? What'll we do now, eh? Where shall we live? Here or Petersburg, eh?

Anna   Oh, St Petersburg, of course. We can't stay here!

Mayor   All right, Petersburg it is. We could do nicely here too, though. Still, to hell with being Mayor, that's what I say, right?

Anna   Oh, a mayor – what's that!

Mayor   I might land a plum job now, what d'you think, my dear? Because if he's hobnobbing with all the Ministers, and goes to court and so on, well, he'll be able to wangle the odd promotion, I could even wind up a general. What d'you reckon, Anna – d'you think I'd make a general?

Anna   Why shouldn't you! Of course you would.

Mayor   Damn me, a general, that'd be marvellous! They hang a sash round your neck, you know, when you get promoted. Which d'you prefer, my dear, the red or the blue?

Anna   Oh, the blue, of course.

Mayor   Eh? You've set your heart on it? Well, the red's fine too. Anyway, d'you know why I fancy being a general? It's because whenever you go somewhere, couriers and adjutants and the like have to gallop on ahead, demanding horses! And they won't let anybody else have them at the staging-posts, they've all got to wait, all these councillors, captains, mayors, and you don't give a damn! You're having dinner with the Governor some place, and it's: 'Stand over there, Mister Mayor!' Hee, hee, hee! (*Goes into fits of laughter.*) Oh yes, that's the real attraction, God damn it!

Anna   You're so coarse, that's you all over. Just bear in mind that we'll have a completely different life, different

friends – no more chasing hares with that dog-mad
judge of yours, and that Zemlyanika creature too. You'll
have new friends, the very last word in refinement,
counts and such like, people with a bit of class. To tell
you the truth, that's the only thing that worries me: you
come out with the odd word now and again, the sort
you'd never hear in polite society.

Mayor   So what? Words never harmed anybody.

Anna   Yes, that's all very well when you were just a
mayor. But this is a completely new life.

Mayor   It is indeed. D'you know they have two
different fish courses? Whitefish and smelts, it makes
your mouth water just looking at them.

Anna   Fish – that's all he thinks about! Well, I want
nothing less than for our house to be the very first in St
Petersburg, and for my room to be dripping with
perfume, so you won't even need to go in, you'll just
stand there with your eyes closed. (*Closes her eyes and
sniffs.*) Mmm, exquisite!

Enter the **Shopkeepers**.

Mayor   Aha! And a good day to you, my brave lads!

Shopkeepers   We wish you good health, Your
Honour.

Mayor   So, my fine fellows, how are things? How's
business, eh? Done complaining, have you, you teapot-
bashers, you tweed-stretchers? The arch-fiddlers, the
prime chisellers, the original short-weight specialists,
complaining about me! Get much out of it, did you? Oh
yes, they'll fling him in jail, you thought. Well, damn
and blast the lot of you, I'll see you in hell first, you
miserable . . .

Anna   Anton, for heaven's sake – your language!

Mayor   (*testily*)   Oh, the hell with that! Listen, you –

that same Government Inspector, the one you were
whingeing to, is marrying my daughter. You didn't know
that, did you, eh? What've you got to say to that, eh?
By God, you're for it now! Swindling innocent people! A
Government contract, to supply rotten cloth – you skim
off a hundred thousand roubles, and you present me
with a measly twenty yards of the stuff – I'm supposed
to give you a medal! By God, if they get to know about
you . . . Oh yes, his gut's sticking out, he must be a
shopkeeper, you can't touch him. 'We're as good as any
aristocrat,' he says. Yes, well, an aristocrat – yes, I'm
talking to you, you pig! – an aristocrat's got to study,
and suppose they do whip him at school, at least he'll
learn something useful. But what about you? You start
out thieving, and your master beats you 'cause you don't
know how to swindle right! Ye gods, you're giving short
change before you can even say the 'Our Father'! And
once you've a big enough paunch on you and you've
lined your pockets, my God, the airs and graces of it!
You swill down sixteen samovars of tea a day and think
you're the cat's whiskers! Well, I spit in your eye, d'you
hear, and your damn pretensions too!

Shopkeepers (*bowing and scraping*)   We're very sorry,
Your Honour.

Mayor   Complain about me, would you? Who was it
helped you fiddle the books, when you built that bridge
and charged twenty thousand for the wood, when there
wasn't even a hundred roubles' worth, eh? It was me,
you miserable old goat! Did you forget that? If I point
the finger, I could still get you packed off to Siberia.
What d'you say to that, eh?

A Shopkeeper   Before God, we're truly sorry, Your
Honour! It was the devil put us up to it. And we'll
never complain again, we promise. We'll do anything
you say, only please don't be angry with us!

Mayor   Don't be angry! Oh yes, you're ready to lick

my boots now, and for why? Because I've had a spot of good luck. But if you'd got the upper hand, even slightly, then by God you'd have trampled me into the mud, you swine, and piled logs on top for the hell of it!

Shopkeepers (*bowing to the ground*)   Oh, please, Your Honour, don't ruin us!

Mayor   Don't ruin you! Oh yes, now it's: 'Don't ruin us!', but what was it before, eh? I tell you, for two pins . . . (*Waves his hand dismissively.*) Well, let God forgive you. I've said my piece. I'm not a vindictive man, but you'd better watch your step from now on. This isn't some upper-class nobody I'm marrying my daughter to, so congratulations are in order – you take my meaning? And don't think you can fob me off with a slice of pickled sturgeon or a sugar-loaf . . . Right, clear off.

The **Shopkeepers** *exit. Enter the* **Judge** *and the* **Charities Warden**.

Judge (*still in the doorway*)   Can we believe the rumours, Your Honour? You've had an extraordinary piece of good fortune?

Warden   Sir, permit me to offer my congratulations on your extraordinary good fortune. I was absolutely delighted when I heard. (*Kisses* **Anna**'s *hand.*) Anna Andreevna! (*Kisses* **Marya**'s *hand.*) Marya Antonovna!

Enter **Rastakovsky**, *a local dignitary*.

Rastakovsky   Congratulations, Your Honour! May God grant you and the happy couple long life and abundant posterity – grandchildren and great-grandchildren! (*Kisses* **Anna**'s *hand.*) Anna Andreevna! (*Kisses* **Marya**'s *hand.*) Marya Antonovna!

Enter **Korobkin**, *and his* **wife**, *and* **Lyulyukov**.

Korobkin   Your Honour, allow me to congratulate you! Anna Andreevna! (*Kisses* **Anna**'s *hand.*) Marya

Antonovna! (*Kisses* **Marya***'s hand.*)

Wife   Anna Andreevna, I most sincerely congratulate you on your good fortune!

Lyulyukov   Congratulations, Anna Andreevna! (*Kisses* **Anna***'s hand, then turns to the audience, clucks his tongue in mock-admiration.*) Marya Antonovna! Congratulations! (*Kisses her hand, then makes the same impudent gesture.*)

Enter numerous visitors in tails and frock-coats, who first kiss **Anna***'s hand, crying: 'Anna Andreevna!', then* **Marya***'s hand, crying: 'Marya Antonovna!' Enter* **Bobchinsky** *and* **Dobchinsky***, jostling for position.*

Bobchinsky   Allow me to offer my congratulations!

Dobchinsky   Your Honour, allow me to offer my congratulations!

Bobchinsky   On this most propitious occasion!

Dobchinsky   Anna Andreevna!

Bobchinsky   Anna Andreevna! (*They bend to kiss her hand simultaneously and bump their foreheads.*)

Dobchinsky   Marya Antonovna! (*Kisses her hand.*) Allow me to congratulate you. You'll be ever so happy, taking the air in a gold dress, and tasting all kinds of dainty dishes. You'll spend your time most agreeably, and . . .

Bobchinsky (*interrupting*)   Marya Antonovna, allow me to congratulate you! May God grant you prosperity, heaps of roubles, and a teeny little baby boy, this high! (*Demonstrates.*) Yes, so small you can sit him on the palm of your hand! And the little scamp'll cry non-stop: Wah! Wah! Wah!

Enter several more visitors, among them the **Superintendent of Schools** *and his* **wife***. They all kiss the ladies' hands.*

Superintendent   Allow me to . . .

His wife (*rushing ahead*)   To offer you my

congratulations, Anna Andreevna! (*They kiss.*) I'm
absolutely overjoyed. 'Anna Andreevna's daughter's
getting married,' they said. 'Good heavens!' I thought,
and I was so delighted I said to my husband: 'Just listen
to this, Luka my dear – Anna Andreevna's had such a
stroke of luck!' 'Well,' I thought, 'thank God for that!'
And I said to him: 'I'm so thrilled for her, I can't wait
to tell Anna Andreevna in person!' 'Oh, heavens above,'
I thought, 'that's just what Anna Andreevna's been
waiting for, a good match for her daughter, and now
look what's happened: she's got exactly what she
wanted.' Yes, I was so overjoyed I couldn't even speak, I
just cried and cried, sobbing my heart out. And Luka
says: 'Nastasya my dear, what are you sobbing for?'
'Oh, dearest Luka,' I says, 'I don't know myself, the
tears just come flooding out.'

Mayor Ladies and gentlemen, please be seated! Hey,
Mishka, bring some more chairs in here.

The visitors sit down. Enter the **Police Chief** *and the*
Constables.

Police Chief Allow me to congratulate you, Your
Excellency, and wish you many long years of prosperity!

Mayor Thank you, thank you! Ladies and gentlemen,
please sit down!

The visitors settle themselves down.

Judge Now tell us, please, Your Honour, how all this
came about – blow by blow, the whole affair.

Mayor Well, it's an extraordinary business: he actually
proposed in person, on the spot.

Anna Oh, but so respectfully, and in the most refined
manner. And he put everything so well – quite
extraordinary: 'Anna Andreevna,' he says, 'I do this
entirely out of respect for your merits . . .' Such a
handsome, well-educated man, a man of the most noble

principles! 'Believe me, Anna Andreevna, life isn't worth a kopeck to me, the only thing I esteem is you, your rare qualities . . .'

Marya Mama, for heaven's sake! It was me he said that to!

Anna You be quiet – you know nothing about it, it's none of your business anyway. 'I'm quite overwhelmed, Anna Andreevna . . .' Really, the compliments he showered on me . . . and just when I was going to say: 'We dare not presume to such an honour,' he suddenly went down on his knees, and said, with the utmost refinement: 'Anna Andreevna, please don't make me the most wretched of men! Consent to requite my love, or I shall put an end to my life!'

Marya Mama, for pity's sake, it was me he was talking about!

Anna Well, of course it was. It was about you too, I'm not denying it.

Mayor He had us scared stiff, you know, said he was going to shoot himself. 'I'll shoot myself!' he says. 'I'll shoot myself!'

Visitors Heavens above!

Judge Fancy that!

Superintendent It's destiny, that's what it is, the workings of fate.

Warden Fate my foot, sir! It's a just reward for honourable service. (*Aside.*) Trust that swine to have all the luck!

Judge I dare say I could sell you that pup, Your Honour, the one you were enquiring about.

Mayor No, I can't be bothered with pups now.

Judge If you don't want that one, we could

agree on another.

Korobkin's wife Oh, Anna Andreevna, you can't imagine how delighted I am at your good fortune!

Korobkin May one ask where our distinguished guest is at present? I heard he'd left town.

Mayor Yes, he's gone off for a day on some extremely urgent business.

Anna Actually to his uncle, to ask his blessing.

Mayor That's right, to ask his blessing. However, tomorrow, without fail . . . (*He sneezes. 'Bless you!' on all sides, merging into a chorus.*) Thank you very much. Anyway, tomorrow without fail . . . (*Sneezes again, another unison chorus, some voices audible above the clamour.*)

Police Chief Good health, Your Excellency!

Dobchinsky God grant you a long and happy life!

Bobchinsky A hundred years and pots of money!

Warden Drop dead!

Korobkin's wife Hell mend you!

Mayor Thank you kindly, sirs. And I wish you the same.

Anna We're planning to move to Petersburg now. I mean, frankly, the air here's so . . . well, it's so provincial. It's quite unpleasant, to be honest. And you see, my husband . . . well, they're going to make him a general.

Mayor That's true, sirs. God damn it, I don't half fancy being a general!

Superintendent Pray God they make you one, Your Honour!

Rastakovsky With God, all things are possible.

Judge   Big ships need deep waters.

Warden   It's in recognition of your service, sir.

Judge (*aside*)   That'll be the day, if they ever make him a general! It'd be like sticking a saddle on a cow! No no, my friend, you're not there yet, not by a long shot. There are plenty with cleaner hands than you, and they still haven't made general.

Warden (*aside*)   Damn the man, who'd believe it – promoting himself to general next! And I wouldn't be surprised if he did it. He's so bumptious the devil himself wouldn't take him! (*Aloud, to the* **Mayor**.) You won't forget us now, will you, Your Honour?

Judge   I mean, if anything turned up, some sort of business matter needing attention, say, we could still count on your support?

Korobkin   I'm taking my boy to Petersburg next year, Your Honour, to put him into the Government service, and I'd be much obliged if you'd use your influence, stand *in loco parentis*, as it were, to the poor little lad.

Mayor   I shall do everything in my power.

Anna   Anton dear, you're too ready to make promises. For a start, you won't even have time to think about these things, and in any case, why on earth should you burden yourself with promises?

Mayor   Well, why not, my dear? I might have the odd spare moment.

Anna   Yes, I daresay, but you can't go using your influence on behalf of every sort of riff-raff.

Korobkin's wife   Did you hear that? Did you hear what she called us?

Woman   Oh, she's always been like that. I know her. Sit a pig at table and she'll show you her trotters!

Enter the **Postmaster**, *out of breath, and clutching a letter with the seal broken.*

Postmaster Oh, sirs! A most extraordinary thing! That fellow we took for a Government Inspector wasn't an Inspector after all!

All What d'you mean – wasn't an Inspector?

Postmaster He wasn't an Inspector at all – it says so in this letter.

Mayor What? What are you talking about? Says so in what letter?

Postmaster This letter he wrote himself, in his own hand. Somebody brings it in to post, I have a look at the address, I see: 'To Post Office Street'. Well, I was thunderstruck. 'He must've found some irregularity in our postal system,' I think to myself, 'and he's reporting us to the authorities.' So I took it and opened it.

Mayor How could you do such a thing!

Postmaster I don't know myself, Your Honour, some supernatural power made me do it. I was just on the point of calling for the courier, to send it off express delivery, but curiosity got the better of me, I swear I've never felt anything like it. 'I can't do it, I can't!' I hear a voice telling me I can't, but something keeps drawing me on! In one ear, I'm hearing: 'Don't dare open that letter, or your goose is cooked!' But in the other ear it's as if some devil's whispering: 'Open it, go on, open it up!' When I pressed down on the sealing-wax, it was as if fire was shooting through my veins, but when I broke it open, honest to God, they were like ice, absolute ice! And my hands were trembling, I nearly passed out.

Mayor Good God, man, how dare you open the letter of such an important personage!

Postmaster Well, that's just it, you see – he's not important, and he's not a personage!

Mayor   So what do you suppose he is, then?

Postmaster   Well, he's nothing in particular – God knows what he is.

Mayor (*incensed*)   Nothing in particular! How dare you call him nothing in particular, yes, and God knows what, besides! I'll have you arrested.

Postmaster   Who, you?

Mayor   Yes, me!

Postmaster   You can't touch me.

Mayor   I'll have you know he's marrying my daughter, which'll make *me* a personage, and I'll ship you off to Siberia!

Postmaster   Siberia's a long way off, Mister Mayor. You'd better wait till I read this. Well, sirs – shall I read this letter?

All   Yes, yes, go on, read it!

Postmaster (*reads*)   'My dear Tryapichkin, I write in haste to inform you of the wonders that have befallen me. On the way out here, an infantry captain took me to the cleaners, and the innkeeper was on the point of flinging me in jail, when suddenly the entire town, on account of my Petersburg looks and dress, mistook me for some Governor-General. Anyway, I'm now living off the fat of the the land at the Mayor's house, making desperate advances to his wife and daughter – the only thing being I can't make up my mind which to start with. I think I'll start with the mother first, she looks game for anything. Do you remember when we were down on our luck, trying to fiddle free dinners, and the pastry-cook nearly frogmarched me out, for charging the pies we'd eaten to the King of England's account? Well, it's a different story now. They're all lending me money here, as much as I want. Honestly you'd die laughing, they're such absolute cretins. I know you write the odd

article: you really should put them in your repertoire.
The Mayor, for a start, is as thick as two short
planks . . .'

Mayor   That's rubbish! It doesn't say that.

Postmaster (*shows him the letter*)   Read it yourself!

Mayor   'Two short planks . . .' No, it's not possible.
You must've written this.

Postmaster   So how could I have written it?

Warden   Read on!

Superintendent   Yes, read on!

Postmaster (*continues*)   'The Mayor is as thick as two
short planks . . .'

Mayor   God damn it, do you need to repeat it! As if
we hadn't heard that already.

Postmaster (*continues*)   Hm . . . hm . . . hm . . .
'. . . two short planks. The Postmaster's a decent chap
too . . .' (*Pauses.*) Well, really! He's been rather rude
about me too.

Mayor   Well, go on, read it out!

Postmaster   But what's the point?

Mayor   Damn it to hell, if you're going to read it, do
so! Read the lot!

Warden   Give it here, I'll read it. (*Puts on his spectacles
and reads.*) 'The Postmaster's the absolute spit of old
Mikheev, our office doorman. I'll bet he's a villain
besides, he drinks like a fish.'

Postmaster (*to the audience*)   Nasty young pup, he needs
a good thrashing!

Warden (*continues*)   'And as for the Charities Warden,
he . . . he . . . he . . .'

Korobkin   What've you stopped for?

Warden   Actually, the writing's terrible ... anyway, the man's obviously a scoundrel.

Korobkin   Give it to me! My eyes are better than yours. (*Tries to take the letter.*)

Warden (*not releasing it*)   It's all right, we can skip this bit, it's much clearer further down.

Korobkin   Come on, hand it over, I've seen it now.

Warden   No no, I'll read it myself. Honestly, the next bit's quite legible.

Postmaster   No, read the whole thing! It's all been read out up to now.

All   Come on, Artemy, hand it over! (*To* **Korobkin**.) Go on, Korobkin, you read it.

Warden   Oh, all right. (*Gives him the letter.*) There you are ... (*Covers part of it with his finger.*) Read on from here. (*They all crowd round.*)

Postmaster   Read it, read it! And no nonsense, mind – read the whole lot!

Korobkin (*reads*)   'And as for the Charities Warden, he's a perfect pig in a skull-cap ...'

Warden (*to the audience*)   It's not even witty! A pig in a skull-cap! Honestly, who ever heard of a pig in a skull-cap?

Korobkin (*continues*)   'And the Schools Superintendent positively reeks of onions ...'

Superintendent (*to the audience*)   I swear to God I've never put an onion in my mouth!

Judge (*aside*)   Well, thank God, at least there's nothing about me!

Korobkin (*reads*)   'The Judge ...'

Judge   Damn! (*Aloud.*) Really, sirs, this letter's far too long. I mean, we don't need to read all this rubbish, do we?

Superintendent   Oh yes we do!

Postmaster   Read it!

Warden   Read the thing!

Korobkin (*continues*)   'The Judge, who goes by the name of Lyapkin-Tyapkin, is the absolute last word in *mauvais ton . . .*' (*Pauses.*) I suppose that's French.

Judge   Yes, and God knows what it means! It's bad enough being called a crook, but that's maybe even worse!

Korobkin (*continues reading*)   'Anyway, they're a most hospitable and generous lot. Goodbye for now, my dear Tryapichkin. I think I'll follow your lead and take up the pen. It's a bit of a bore, living like this – a fellow needs some sustenance for the soul, after all. You've got to put your mind to higher things, that's how I see it. You can write to me at Podkatilovka, that's in Saratov province . . .' (*Turns over the letter and reads the address.*) 'To the Honorable Ivan Vasilievich Tryapichkin, third floor right, No. 97 Post Office Street, St Petersburg.'

A Lady   Well, that was completely out of the blue!

Mayor   He's cut my throat, the swine! I'm dead, I'm finished! I can't see a damn thing, nothing but pigs' snouts – no faces, just pigs' snouts. Get him back here, right now! (*Flapping his arms.*)

Postmaster   Fat chance! I told our stationmaster to give him the best team of horses we'd got, made a point of it. Damned if I didn't even give him clearance right through to Saratov.

Korobkin's wife   What a mess! What a frightful carry-on!

Judge   Yes, well, damn it to hell, sirs – I lent him three hundred roubles!

Warden   He's got three hundred roubles of mine too!

Postmaster (*sighs*)   And mine.

Bobchinsky   Plus sixty-five in notes, from Dobchinsky and me, sirs, oh yes.

Judge (*spreading his hands helplessly*)   Gentlemen, gentlemen, how could this happen? How could we make such idiots of ourselves?

Mayor (*slapping his forehead*)   How could I, you mean? I must be going senile. I've outlived my wits, like some stupid old goat. Thirty years I've been in the service, and not one shopkeeper, not one contractor, could ever get the better of me. Top-flight villains, crooks who could swindle other crooks, I've outsmarted the lot of them, fiddlers and fixers, people who could walk off with the world, I've reeled them all in. Dear God, I've hoodwinked three Governors! Governors, huh! (*Waves his hand in disgust.*) Don't get me started on Governors.

Anna   But Anton dearest, it's not possible: he's engaged to our Masha . . .

Mayor (*furious*)   Engaged! Engaged my arse! Don't talk to me about engagement! That was just another damn trick, to pull the wool over my eyes. (*In a frenzy.*) Just look at me, eh? Let the whole world, the whole of Christendom, have a good look, see what an ass the Mayor's made of himself! Idiot! Cretin! Stupid old fool! (*Shakes his fist at himself.*) Hey, you! Fat nose! You took that miserable little squirt for a big cheese! Well, he'll be telling it with bells on now, the whole road home! He'll broadcast his story to every corner of the globe. And if that's not bad enough, being made a laughing-stock, some hack, some wretched scribbler'll come along and stick you in a comedy. That's what really hurts! He'll spare nobody, rank and title count for nothing, and they'll all sit grinning and clapping their hands. So what are you laughing at, eh? You're laughing at yourselves, that's what! Oh, you! (*Stamps his foot in rage.*) By God, if I could get my hands on those scribblers! Penpushers! Damn liberals! Devil's spawn! By God, I'd tie the whole lot of you up in a bundle and grind you to powder! I'd stuff you into the lining of the devil's cap! (*Lashes out with his fist and stamps his heel on the floor. A brief silence, then.*) I still can't think straight. I mean, people God wants to punish, he first sends them mad, right? So what was there about this nitwit that remotely resembled a Government Inspector? Not a damn thing! Not so much as the tip of his miserable finger! But suddenly it's all Inspector this, Inspector that! Who first gave out that he was an Inspector, eh? Come on, answer me!

Warden (*spreading his arms*)   For the life of me, I can't explain how it happened. It was as if some sort of fog came down on us, the devil must've led us astray.

Judge   Well, I know who started it! It was those two, they started it, those fine specimens there! (*Points to* **Dobchinsky** *and* **Bobchinsky**.)

Bobchinsky   Hold on, hold on! It wasn't me! I never dreamed . . .

Dobchinsky   I never said a thing . . .

Warden   It was you two all right!

Superintendent   Of course it was! You came running in here from the inn like madmen: 'He's here! He's here, and he's not paying his bill!' Oh yes, you found your big cheese all right!

Mayor   It just had to be you, hadn't it! The town gossips! Damn scandalmongers!

Warden   Damn you to hell, both of you, with your Government Inspector and your stupid stories!

Mayor   You do nothing but snoop around the town,

upsetting everybody, you blabbermouths! Dishing the dirt, like a couple of chattering magpies!

Judge   Layabouts!

Superintendent   Fatheads!

Warden   Potbellied runts!

They all start to surround them.

Bobchinsky   Oh God, it wasn't me, it was Pyotr Ivanovich!

Dobchinsky   No, it wasn't, it was you, Pyotr Ivanovich, you started . . .

Bobchinsky   It was not! It was you that started . . .

Enter a **Gendarme**.

Gendarme   Gentlemen! A Government Inspector, appointed by decree of His Imperial Majesty, has just arrived from St Petersburg, and is staying at the inn, where you are to proceed forthwith.

At these words, they are thunderstruck. Cries of astonishment from the ladies, uttered simultaneously. The whole company then suddenly changes position and freezes on the spot, as if turned to stone.

Dumb show. The **Mayor** *stands in the centre, like a pillar, with his arms outstretched and his head flung back. To the right are his* **Wife** *and* **Daughter**, *their entire bodies straining towards him; behind them stands the* **Postmaster**, *transformed into a sort of question mark, facing the audience; behind him stands the* **Schools Superintendent**, *with a look of helpless innocence; behind him, and at the far side of the stage, three visiting ladies, leaning against one another with the most satirical expression on their faces, are looking straight at the* **Mayor**'s *family. To the left of the* **Mayor** *stands the* **Charities Warden**, *his head cocked to one side as if straining to listen; behind him, the* **Judge**, *with his arms stuck out, is practically squatting on the floor, and moving his lips, as if trying to whistle, or utter the* words: 'Here's another fine mess!' Behind him, **Korobkin**, facing the audience, with his eyes screwed up, directs a look of contempt at the **Mayor**; and behind him again, at the other side of the stage, stand **Bobchinsky** and **Dobchinsky**, their arms outflung towards each other, open-mouthed and goggle-eyed. The other guests stand around like pillars. The petrified company maintain their position for almost a minute and a half. Then the curtain is lowered.

Marriage

*A thoroughly improbable event
in two acts*

Characters

Agafya Tikhonovna, *a merchant's daughter, the bride-to-be*
Arina Panteleimonovna, *her aunt*
Fyokla Ivanovna, *a matchmaker*
Podkolyosin, *a court councillor (seventh-grade civil servant)*
Kochkaryov, *his friend*
Omelet, *an office manager*
Anuchkin, *a retired infantry officer*
Zhevakin, *a naval officer*
Dunyashka, *a serving maid*
Starikov, *a shopkeeper*
Stepan, *Podkolyosin's manservant*

Act One

Scene One

The scene is a bachelor's apartment. **Podkolyosin** *is alone, stretched out on a settee, smoking a pipe.*

Podkolyosin Yes, when you're on your own, sitting around thinking, you realise it's time you were married. What's it all for, anyway? You go on and on, just living, till you're absolutely sick of it. That's another season I've let slip by. Yet everything seemed all set, the matchmaker's been coming for three months now – honestly, I'm ashamed of myself. Hey, Stepan!

Stepan *enters.*

Podkolyosin Hasn't the matchmaker arrived yet?

Stepan No, sir.

Podkolyosin Have you been to the tailor?

Stepan Yes, sir.

Podkolyosin Is he working on my frock-coat?

Stepan He is, sir.

Podkolyosin How far has he got?

Stepan Quite far, sir – he's onto the buttonholes now.

Podkolyosin What did you say?

Stepan I said, he's onto the buttonholes now.

Podkolyosin Didn't he ask what your master needed the coat for?

Stepan No, he didn't.

Podkolyosin Didn't he say, 'Is your master thinking of getting married, perhaps?'

Stepan   No, he didn't say anything.

Podkolyosin   But you did see some other frock-coats in the shop, didn't you? I mean, he is making them for other people?

Stepan   Yes, he's got lots of coats hanging up.

Podkolyosin   But I daresay they're not as good quality cloth as mine, right?

Stepan   Oh no, sir, yours looks much smarter.

Podkolyosin   What did you say?

Stepan   I said, yours looks much smarter.

Podkolyosin   Good. So, didn't he ask why your master was having a coat made of such fine cloth?

Stepan   No, sir.

Podkolyosin   What, he didn't say, is your master getting married, by any chance?

Stepan   No, he didn't say a word about that.

Podkolyosin   I presume you told him my rank, and where I work?

Stepan   I did.

Podkolyosin   And what did he say to that?

Stepan   He said, 'I'll do my best.'

Podkolyosin   All right. Off you go. (**Stepan** *exits*.) Hm, a black coat is more dignified, to my way of thinking. Coloured coats are for secretaries, low-grade clerks and suchlike, weedy types basically. Higher-ranking people like us have to pay more attention, as they say, to ... oh, damn, I've forgotten the word. It's such a good word, too, and I can't remember it. Yes, by God, you can say what you like, but a court councillor's equivalent to a colonel, without the epaulettes on the uniform, of course. Hey, Stepan!

Stepan *enters.*

Stepan   Yes, sir?

Podkolyosin   Did you buy the shoe-polish?

Stepan   Yes, sir.

Podkolyosin   Where did you get it? Did you buy it in that little shop I told you about, on Voznesensky Prospect?

Stepan   Yes, sir, I did.

Podkolyosin   And is it good stuff?

Stepan   Yes, sir.

Podkolyosin   Have you tried it on my boots?

Stepan   I have, sir.

Podkolyosin   And do they shine?

Stepan   They certainly do, sir.

Podkolyosin   And when he was letting you have the polish – didn't he ask what your master needed it for?

Stepan   No.

Podkolyosin   Are you sure he didn't say, 'Is your master thinking of getting married?'

Stepan   No, he didn't say anything.

Podkolyosin   All right, fine. Off you go. (**Stepan** *exits.*) Yes, boots might seem a trivial matter, but if they're poorly made, and the polish is rusty, you'll get no respect in the best society. Nothing looks right. And what's even worse is if they give you corns. If there's one thing I can't stand it's corns. Hey, Stepan!

Stepan *enters.*

Stepan   Your honour?

Podkolyosin   You told the shoemaker I didn't want corns?

Stepan   Yes, sir.

Podkolyosin   And what did he say?

Stepan   He said, 'All right.' (*Exits.*)

Podkolyosin   Yes, marriage is a damnably tricky business! If it's not one thing, it's another. Everything's got to be just right, and that's no easy matter, whatever they say. Hey, Stepan! (**Stepan** *enters.*) There's something else I meant to tell you . . .

Stepan   Sir, the old woman's here.

Podkolyosin   Ah, she's here – send her in. (**Stepan** *exits.*) Yes, it's a business all right . . . it's not what you'd . . . it's damn tricky.

Fyokla *enters.*

Podkolyosin   Good morning, good morning, Fyokla Ivanovna! Well, now, how are things? Pull up a chair, sit down, please, and tell me. So, how is everything going? What's her name again? Melanya?

Fyokla   Agafya Tikhonovna.

Podkolyosin   Yes, yes, of course – Agafya. Most likely some old maid in her forties.

Fyokla   Heavens, no, sir. You marry her, and you'll be singing her praises night and day, you'll thank me, and that's a fact.

Podkolyosin   A likely story!

Fyokla   I'm too long in the tooth for stories, dear sir. Mongrels tell stories.

Podkolyosin   What about her dowry? Yes, the dowry – tell me again about the dowry.

Fyokla   Well, as to her dowry, there's a stone house in the city, Moscow district, two storeys, a real goldmine it is, a joy to behold. The grain-merchant alone pays seven hundred roubles for his shop. And the beer cellar in the basement pulls in a fair crowd. There are two wood-built extensions – one of them's all wood, the other's on a stone foundation – they bring in about four hundred roubles each. There's an allotment, too, in the Vyborg area: a shopkeeper rented it to grow cabbage a couple of years ago, he's teetotal, never touches a drop, and he's got three sons. He's already married off two of them, but the third's still young, he says, he can stay in the shop, lighten the load a bit. 'I'm an old man,' he says, 'the boy can stay in the shop, take some of the weight off me.'

Podkolyosin But what about the girl, what does she look like?

Fyokla Oh, an absolute sugar lump! Peaches-and-cream complexion, so sweet you couldn't describe her. You'll be struck dumb, sir. You'll be so happy with her (*Demonstrates how much.*) you'll tell all your friends, and even your enemies – this is all thanks to Fyokla Ivanovna.

Podkolyosin Yes, but she isn't officer class, is she?

Fyokla Her father's a respectable merchant. And she'd be no disgrace to a general – she won't hear of marrying a shopkeeper. I don't care what my husband's like, she says, even if he's not good-looking, but he's got to be a gentleman. Oh, she's so refined, I tell you! When she puts on her silk dress on Sundays, honest to God, you should hear it rustle! A princess, pure and simple.

Podkolyosin Well, that was why I asked, you see, because I'm a court councillor, and you do understand . . .

Fyokla Of course, of course, I understand. We had another court councillor, and she turned him down, didn't like him at all. He had a very strange habit – couldn't open his mouth without telling a lie, and him a fine-looking gentleman, too. Well, what can you do? That's the way God made him. He's not happy about it himself, but he just can't help lying. It's God's will, so it seems.

Podkolyosin   Anyway, apart from this girl, have you any others?

Fyokla   Heavens, what more do you want? You couldn't find a better.

Podkolyosin   So, she's the best you've got?

Fyokla   Sir, if you travelled the world over, you wouldn't find her equal.

Podkolyosin   Well, I'll think about it, I'll give it some thought. Drop by the day after tomorrow and we'll do the same. I'll have a lie-down and you can tell me . . .

Fyokla   Please, sir! I've been coming here now for three months and there's nothing to show for it. All you do is sit around in your dressing-gown, puffing on that pipe of yours.

Podkolyosin   I suppose you think marriage is easy – that it's like shouting: 'Hey, Stepan, bring me my boots!' You just pull them on and go! But it's not, you've got to think hard, look very carefully.

Fyokla   Listen, if you want to have a look, then do so. That's what the goods are there for, to be looked at. Tell your man to fetch your coat and we'll go right now, while it's still morning.

Podkolyosin   What, now? Look at the clouds – if we go out now we'll get caught in the rain, for sure.

Fyokla   Well, that's your hard luck. Good God, sir, you're going grey already, soon you won't even be fit to do a husband's business. Huh, turns up his nose because he's a court councillor! Well, we'll find plenty of suitors, don't you worry, and a sight better than you!

Podkolyosin   What nonsense is this? What on earth do you mean, I'm going grey? Where do you see a grey hair? Eh? (*Feels his hair.*)

Fyokla   Of course you've got grey hair, it does happen, you know. So you'd better watch out! Huh, doesn't fancy this one, doesn't fancy that one! Well, I've got my eye on a captain, yes, you wouldn't even come up to his shoulder, and he's got a voice like a trumpet. He works in that what's-its-name – Admiralty, yes.

Podkolyosin   You're talking rubbish – I'm going to look in the mirror, see just where this grey hair's supposed to be. Hey, Stepan, bring in a mirror! No, never mind, I'll get it myself. Grey hairs! God help us, that's worse than the pox! (*Exits to the adjoining room.*)

Kochkaryov *enters in a hurry.*

Kochkaryov   Where's Podkolyosin? (*Catching sight of* **Fyokla**.) What are you doing here? Listen, you ... why the hell did you talk me into getting married?

Fyokla   What's wrong with that? You did your duty.

Kochkaryov   Did my duty! And I'm rewarded with a wife? I couldn't have managed without one, could I?

Fyokla   It was you that came pestering me – find me a wife, granny, that's all I kept hearing.

Kochkaryov   You sly old hag! Anyway, what are you doing here? Don't tell me Podkolyosin's thinking of ...

Fyokla   And why not? If it's God's will.

Kochkaryov   Seriously? The wretch hasn't even mentioned it. Well, isn't he just the one? Thought he'd keep it dark, eh?

Podkolyosin *enters, holding a mirror, which he is peering into intently.*

Podkolyosin   So where's this grey hair you're raving about? There's nothing of the sort.

Kochkaryov (*creeps up behind him*)   Boo!

Podkolyosin (*shrieks and drops the mirror*)   Oh! You madman! What the hell . . . That's really stupid – you just about frightened the life out of me.

Kochkaryov   Take it easy, it was only a joke.

Podkolyosin   Huh, some joke. I still can't get over it – you scared me half to death. And I've broken the mirror, look. It wasn't a cheap item, either – that was out of the English shop.

Kochkaryov   Oh, forget it – I'll get you a new one.

Podkolyosin   Oh yes, I know these new mirrors of yours – you look ten years older in them, your face comes out all squint.

Kochkaryov   Listen, it's me that should be angry with you. We're supposed to be friends, and you've been keeping a secret from me all this time. You're thinking of getting married, right?

Podkolyosin   That's rubbish. It's never entered my mind.

Kochkaryov   What? The proof's here, staring me in the face. (*Points to* **Fyokla**.) I mean, we all know what kind of bird she is. Oh, come on, come on – there's nothing wrong with that. It's a Christian act – a patriotic duty, even. Listen, leave it to me, I'll take care of everything. (*To* **Fyokla**.) Right then, tell me – who, what, and all the rest. What's her family – nobility, civil service, merchant? And what's her name?

Fyokla   Agafya – Agafya Tikhonovna.

Kochkaryov   Brandakhlystova?

Fyokla   No – Kuperdyagina.

Kochkaryov   Right – lives in Six Shops Street, is that the one?

Fyokla   No no – nearer the Sands, in Soap Lane.

Kochkaryov   Oh, of course – Soap Lane, the wooden house at the back of the shop . . .

Fyokla   No, not that one – the one behind the beer-cellar.

Kochkaryov   Behind the beer-cellar? No, I don't know it.

Fyokla   Well, when you turn up the lane, there's a sentry-box just facing, and you go past that and turn left, and it's right in front of you, you can't miss it – I mean, it's the wooden house that's directly in front of you – that's where the dressmaker stays, she used to live with the Chief Secretary to the Senate. Of course, you're not looking for the dressmaker, but right behind her there'll be another house, a stone one, and that's hers – that's the house Agafya Tikhonovna stays in, our young lady.

Kochkaryov   Good, good. Right, I'll attend to all this, and you can go. You're not needed any longer.

Fyokla   What d'you mean? You're surely not going to arrange the wedding yourself?

Kochkaryov   Yes, yes, of course – just you keep out of the way.

Fyokla   Oh! The cheek of it! This isn't a job for a man, you know. You'd better stay out of it, I'm telling you.

Kochkaryov   Go on, off you go. You haven't a clue, anyway. Don't interfere, just mind your own business. Now, clear off.

Fyokla Godless creature – stealing the bread out of other people's mouths! Really, getting mixed up in this carry-on. By God, if I'd known, I wouldn't have said a word. (*Exits in high dudgeon.*)

Kochkaryov Now, my friend, you can't put this off any longer – let's go!

Podkolyosin But I'm still not sure. I've only just had the idea . . .

Kochkaryov Oh, nonsense, nonsense! Don't hang back, that's all – I'll marry you off so fast you won't feel a thing! We'll drive over to see this young woman, and do it right now, quick as a flash.

Podkolyosin What, now? That's all I need.

Kochkaryov Why on earth not? What's keeping you? I mean, just look at yourself – you see what comes of not being married? Take a look at your room – what's in it? One muddy boot over there, a wash-basin here, there's tobacco all over the table, and you're flat on your back all day, like a lounge lizard.

Podkolyosin That's true. There's no order to my life, I know.

Kochkaryov Well, once you're married, you simply won't recognise yourself, or anything else, for that matter. You'll have a nice sofa, a little dog, some sort of canary in a cage, needlework . . . Just imagine – you're sitting on the sofa, and suddenly this delightful girl, very pretty, sits down beside you and places her hand . . .

Podkolyosin Oh, damn! You know, when you come to think of it, they do have lovely hands. They're like milk, they're so soft and white.

Kochkaryov And that's not the half of it! It's not just hands – I tell you, friend, they've got . . . Oh, there's no point even trying – what haven't they got, God only knows!

Podkolyosin Well, to tell you the truth, I do like it when a pretty girl sits beside me.

Kochkaryov There you are, you see? Now all we've got to do is sort out the details. Don't you worry about a thing. I'll organise the wedding dinner and such like – you'll need at least a dozen bottles of champagne, I don't care what you say. And Madeira, a half-dozen, for sure. You can bet the bride'll have a whole gang of aunties and girlfriends, and they don't play games. As for hock, the hell with it, who needs it, eh? Now, on the matter of dinner, I have a caterer in mind – that damn dog'll feed you till you can barely get up from the table.

Podkolyosin Hold on, hold on – you're going on at such a rate, as if the wedding's already been decided.

Kochkaryov And why not? What are you putting it off for? You agreed, didn't you?

Podkolyosin Did I? No, I didn't agree to anything.

Kochkaryov Nonsense! You've just this minute said you wanted to get married.

Podkolyosin No, no, all I said was that it mightn't be a bad idea.

Kochkaryov Now, look here – we were just on the point of . . . What are you saying? Are you telling me you don't fancy married life?

Podkolyosin No, no, I do.

Kochkaryov So what's the matter? What's stopping you?

Podkolyosin Nothing's stopping me. It's just a bit strange, that's all.

Kochkaryov What's strange?

Podkolyosin I don't know, it's a bit odd. I mean, my whole life I've been unmarried, and now suddenly I'm married.

Kochkaryov Oh, come on – you should be
ashamed of yourself. You need a serious talking-to, that's
obvious. Right, I'll speak frankly with you, like father to
son. Just look at yourself – take a good look right now,
for example, at the expression on your face. What are
you, eh? A lump of wood, that's what, you're of no
significance whatsoever. What are you living for, eh?
You look in the mirror and what do you see? A stupid
face, and that's about it. Now, you imagine yourself
having kids, and not just two or three, but maybe a full
half-dozen, and every one your spitting image, like peas
in a pod. You're all on your own now, court councillor,
despatcher, office manager or whatever, God knows –
but just imagine yourself surrounded by tiny little
despatchers, swarms of them, smart little rascals, and one
little imp stretches out his hands, he's going to tug at
your whiskers, and you make doggy noises for him:
grrwowff! grrrwowff! Now, you can't beat that, can you?
Admit it.

Podkolyosin Yes, but they're such brats – they'll spoil
all my things, and scatter all my papers.

Kochkaryov So what if they are brats? They'll look
like you, isn't that enough?

Podkolyosin You know, that's actually quite funny,
damn it – some little dumpling, some smart young pup,
and he's the spitting image of you!

Kochkaryov How couldn't it be funny? Of course it's
funny. Anyway, let's go.

Podkolyosin All right, we'll go.

Kochkaryov Hey, Stepan! Come on, help your
master get dressed.

Podkolyosin (*getting dressed in front of the mirror*) I think
I ought to have a white waistcoat, though.

Kochkaryov   Oh, rubbish, who cares?

Podkolyosin (*trying to put on a stiff collar*)   That damned laundress! She only half-starches these collars, they won't even stand up. Stepan, you tell her from me, if this is how she's going to iron my linen, I'll find somebody else. Spends all her time with her boyfriends, no doubt, instead of getting on with it.

Kochkaryov   Oh, come on, for heaven's sake – stop fussing.

Podkolyosin   I'm coming, I'm coming. (*Puts on his frock-coat and sits down.*) Listen, Ilya, I'll tell you what – why don't you go by yourself?

Kochkaryov   What?! Have you gone mad? Me go? Who is it that's getting married, me or you?

Podkolyosin   To tell you the truth, I don't feel up to it. Maybe tomorrow.

Kochkaryov   Listen, have you got an ounce of brains in your head? Are you an idiot, or what? You're all fixed up to go, and suddenly you don't want to? I mean, tell me, what sort of miserable swine would do a thing like that?

Podkolyosin   What are you shouting at me for? What gives you the right? What have I done to you?

Kochkaryov   You're a fool, sir, an absolute idiot, that's what everybody'll say. You're stupid, yes, stupid, supposing you are a despatcher. I mean, what am I knocking my brains out for? For your benefit, that's what. Otherwise, they'll all beat you to it, you wait and see. Huh, and meanwhile he loafs around, playing the damn bachelor! So you tell me, please, what sort of person you are – a bad lot, frankly, a numskull. I'd call you something else, but decency forbids. You're an old woman! You're worse than an old woman!

Podkolyosin   You're a fine one to talk. (*Sotto voce.*)

Have you taken leave of your senses? Swearing in front of a servant, using words like that, really! Couldn't you find a better place?

Kochkaryov   Well, why shouldn't I swear, answer me that? Who wouldn't swear at you? Who could resist it? You'd drive anybody to swear! I mean, a respectable gentleman decides to get married, to do the sensible thing – then suddenly, out of sheer folly, as if he'd had a brainstorm, starts acting like the village idiot . . .

Podkolyosin   All right, all right, I'll go – there's no need to shout.

Kochkaryov   I'll go, he says! Damn right you'll go, what else can you do?! (*To* **Stepan**.) Bring him his hat and coat.

Podkolyosin (*on his way out*)   Honestly, what a strange fellow. There's no getting along with him – suddenly starts swearing, without any rhyme or reason. Just doesn't know how to behave.

Kochkaryov   Well, that's that. I'm not swearing now. (*They exit.*)

Scene Two

A room in **Agafya Tikhonovna**'s *house.* **Agafya** *is dealing out cards for fortune-telling, while her aunt,* **Arina**, *looks over her shoulder.*

Agafya   It's another journey, Auntie! There's a king of diamonds involved, tears, a love letter; the king of clubs on the left seems very keen, but some wicked woman's getting in the way.

Arina   So who might this king of clubs be, do you think?

Agafya   I don't know.

Arina Well, I do.

Agafya Who?

Arina He's a merchant, a fine man, in the drapery business – Mr Starikov.

Agafya No, I'm sure it's not him – I'd put money on it.

Arina Agafya, don't argue – he's got dark hair, the king of clubs, it can't be anybody else.

Agafya No no, the king of clubs means it's a gentleman – it can't be a shopkeeper, not the king of clubs.

Arina Oh, Agafya, you wouldn't have said that if your poor dear father was still alive. The way old Tikhon used to bang his fist on the table, and shout: 'I'd spit on any man who's ashamed of being a merchant,' he'd say, 'I wouldn't give my daughter to a colonel! Other people can do what they like,' he'd say, 'I won't let my son even enter the service! Surely a merchant serves the Tsar as well as anybody else?' And then he'd crash his fist down on the table. He'd a hand on him the size of a bucket, and what a temper! To tell you the truth, he was the death of your dear mother – she'd have lived a bit longer, but for him.

Agafya There, you see? That's all I need, a bad-tempered husband like that. No, I wouldn't marry a shopkeeper at any price.

Arina Well, Mr Starikov's nothing like that.

Agafya I don't want him – he's got a beard. When he eats, it all dribbles down his chin. I won't have him, absolutely not.

Arina So where are you going to find a nice gentleman? They don't grow on trees, you know.

Agafya Fyokla Ivanovna's going to find me one. She

promised she'd come up with the very best.

Arina But she's a terrible liar, my darling.

Fyokla *enters.*

Fyokla Oh, Arina! Don't you know it's a sin to slander people? That's wicked.

Agafya Why, it's Fyokla Ivanovna! Now, tell me, please – have you found one?

Fyokla Yes, yes – just let me catch my breath! Honestly, the trouble I've been to! I've been through every house in town on your business, trailing round offices, ministries, hanging outside army barracks . . . d'you know, my dear, I almost got beaten up! I swear to God, that old woman that matched up the Aferovs practically flew at me! 'You old so-and-so,' she says, 'you're taking the bread out of our mouths. Stick to your own patch!' Well, I just told her straight out, I says, 'I'll do anything to satisfy my young lady, so don't go getting angry at me!' Anyway, wait till you see the gentlemen I've got in store for you! I tell you, there's been nothing like them since the dawn of time! And they're coming here this very day, some of them! I've run on ahead to warn you.

Agafya Today? Oh, Fyokla Ivanovna, my dear, I'm frightened!

Fyokla Don't be afraid, dear lady, it's the usual thing. They'll come and give you the once-over, that's all. And you can have a look at them. If you don't like what you see, well, let them leave.

Arina Huh – it'll be a fine bunch you've roped in, no doubt!

Agafya So how many are there? A lot?

Fyokla Indeed, there's six of them.

Agafya (*shrieks*) Ooh!

Fyokla Now, what are you getting in such a flap for, my dear? It's better to have a choice – if one doesn't suit, another will.

Agafya But are they gentlemen?

Fyokla They are, hand-picked, every one. I tell you, you've never seen such gentlemen.

Agafya So what are they like then?

Fyokla Wonderful! So handsome, and very smart. The first one's Baltazar – Mr Zhevakin – terribly good-looking, he served in the navy – he's just up your street. Word is, he likes 'em on the plump side, can't be doing with skinny women. Then there's Ivan Pavlovich, a civil servant, he's so high up you can't even get in to see him. A fine-looking gentleman, too, quite stout – yes, and he shouts at me, he says, 'Now don't give me any of your nonsense – the young lady's this or that – just tell me straight out, how much she's worth in property and movables.' 'This much here, that much there, my dear,' I says. 'You're a lying cow!' he says, yes, and he stuck in another word, dear lady, it wouldn't be proper to repeat. Well, I could see right away, he must be an important gentleman.

Agafya So who else is there?

Fyokla Well, there's Mr Anuchkin. He's so refined, dear lady, and his lips – like raspberries, perfect raspberries – a delightful man. 'I want my bride,' he says, 'to be good-looking, and well brought-up, and she's got to be able to speak French.' Oh yes, my dear – a most particular person, bit of the German about him – such a delicate creature, and such lovely slender legs.

Agafya Mm . . . I'm not keen on these delicate types – something not quite . . . oh, I don't know, I don't see much in them.

Fyokla Well, if you want something a bit more solid,

then take Ivan Pavlovich. You couldn't choose better.
Now, he's a real gentleman, if anybody is. Why, you'd
scarcely get him through that door – a fine figure of a
man.

Agafya How old is he?

Fyokla He's still a young man – mm ... fiftyish, but
not fifty yet.

Agafya And what's his last name again?

Fyokla Er ... his family name's Omelet.

Agafya What? What sort of name's that?

Fyokla Just a name.

Agafya Good God, what a name! I mean, really,
Fyokla – if I marry him I'll be called Mrs Omelet – ye
gods, the very idea!

Fyokla Well, my dear, there's some damnable names
in Russia – they'd make you spit and cross yourself,
even just to hear them. Still, if you don't fancy the
name, you can take Mr Zhevakin – Baltazar, he's a
wonderful man.

Agafya What kind of hair does he have?

Fyokla Oh, very nice.

Agafya How about his nose?

Fyokla Er ... that's nice too. Everything's where it
should be. He's a splendid person. Only don't be upset,
my dear, but he's got nothing in his flat except his pipe
– not a stick of furniture.

Agafya So who else is there?

Fyokla There's Mr Panteleevich – he's a civil servant,
a titular councillor. He's got a bit of a stammer, but he's
very quiet.

Agafya Why d'you keep going on about civil servants?

Tell me if he drinks, that's more to the point.

Fyokla Well, he does drink, I won't deny it. But he's a titular councillor, my dear, what do you expect? And he's as quiet as a mouse.

Agafya No no, I'm not having him – I don't want a drunkard for a husband.

Fyokla Well, that's up to you, my dear. If you don't want one, then choose another, but I mean, really, what if he does take a drop too much now and again? He isn't drunk the whôle week, you know. Some days he's sober as a judge.

Agafya Right, who's next?

Fyokla Just one more, but he's not very . . . Well, God forgive him, the others are a bit smarter.

Agafya And who is he?

Fyokla I wasn't going to mention him, but if you must know, he's a court councillor, wears a ribbon in his buttonhole and everything. Only he's so hard to shift – you won't even get him across the door.

Agafya So, who else is there? That's five, you said there were six.

Fyokla What, isn't that enough for you? You're getting carried away now, and a minute ago you were scared stiff.

Arina What use are they anyway, these gentlemen of yours, even if there are six of them? One merchant's worth the whole lot.

Fyokla Oh, no, Arina, dear – a gentleman's more respected.

Arina Huh, who needs respect? Just you look at any merchant, bowling along in his sledge, with his sable hat on.

Fyokla Yes but when a gentleman in epaulettes meets up with him, he'll say, 'Who do you think you are, you miserable shopkeeper? Get out of the way!' Or else he'll say, 'Now, shopkeeper, show me your best velvet!' And your merchant'll say, 'Yes, sir, if you please, sir!' And it'll be, 'Take off your hat, you oaf!' Yes, that's what a gentleman'll say.

Arina Yes, well, the merchant won't give him the cloth, if he doesn't want to, so your gentleman'll have to go naked, 'cos he'll have nothing to wear.

Fyokla So the gentleman'll take his sword to the merchant.

Arina And the merchant'll complain to the police.

Fyokla And the gentleman'll complain to the senator.

Arina And the merchant'll complain to the governor.

Fyokla And the gentleman'll . . .

Arina Oh, don't talk rubbish, you and your gentlemen! A governor's higher than a senator! Dear God, how she goes on about her gentlemen – even a gentleman's got to tip his hat at times . . . (*The doorbell rings.*) There's somebody at the door.

Fyokla Oh God, it's them!

Arina Who?

Fyokla It's them – it's one of the suitors. (*Exits.*)

Agafya (*shrieks*) Ooh!

Arina Saints have mercy on us sinners! The room's not even been tidied! (*Snatches up everything from the table and rushes round the room.*) And the cloth, the tablecloth's filthy! Dunyashka! Dunyashka!

Dunyashka *enters.*

Arina Hurry, a clean tablecloth! (*Pulls the cloth off the* *table and bustles about the room.*)

Agafya   Oh, Auntie, what am I going to do? I'm practically in my nightgown!

Arina   Run and get dressed, my dear, hurry!

Continues scurrying round the room. **Dunyashka** *brings a fresh tablecloth. The doorbell rings again.*

Arina   Run and say, 'Just a minute!'

Dunyashka *is heard off-stage: 'Just a minute!'*

Agafya   Auntie, this dress isn't ironed!

Arina   Oh, Lord have mercy on us – put on another!

Fyokla (*rushes in*)   What on earth's keeping you? Agafya, my dear, hurry up, please! (*The doorbell rings again.*) Heavens above, he's still waiting!

Arina   Dunyashka, show him in, and ask him to wait.

Dunyashka *runs into the hall and opens the door. Voices off-stage: 'Is she at home?' 'Oh yes, sir, please come in.' Consumed with curiosity, the women strain to catch a glimpse of him through the keyhole.*

Agafya (*shrieks*)   Oh, he's so fat!

Fyokla   He's coming, he's coming! (*All rush headlong out.*)

Omelet *and* **Dunyashka** *enter.*

Dunyashka   Wait here, please. (*Exits.*)

Omelet   Well, I suppose so, as long as they don't take an age. I've only nipped out of the office for a minute. And if the general takes it into his head to ask 'Where's the manager?' – 'He's gone to check out a young lady' – Well, he'd give me 'young lady' and no mistake! Anyway, I'd better have another look at the inventory . . . (*Reads.*) 'Stone house, two storeys . . .' (*Raises his eyes and has a look round the room.*) Yes. (*Resumes reading.*) 'Two extensions: one on stone foundations, one on

wood ...' Hm ... the wooden one's not up to much. 'A
carriage, a two-horse sleigh with carvings, one large rug,
one small.' Possibly they're only fit for scrap. Still, the
old woman says they're first class – all right, let's say
they are. 'Two dozen silver spoons.' Yes, of course,
you've got to have silver spoons. 'Two fox furs ...'
Hm ... 'Four large quilts, and two small ones ...' (*Purses
his lips meaningfully*.) 'A dozen silk dresses, a dozen cotton,
two nightgowns, two ...' Oh, this is trumpery ...
'Sheets, tablecloths ...' She can do what she likes with
that stuff. I suppose I'd better check it, though. These
days they promise you houses and carriages, then when
you marry them you find nothing but quilts and feather
beds.

The doorbell rings. **Dunyashka** *hurries through the room to
open the door. Voices off-stage: 'Is she at home?' 'Yes, sir.'*
Dunyashka *re-enters with* **Anuchkin**.

Dunyashka   Wait here, sir. They're just coming.
(*Exits.*)

Anuchkin *and* **Omelet** *exchange bows.*

Omelet   Good day, sir.

Anuchkin   Tell me, sir, have I not the honour of
addressing the young lady's dear papa?

Omelet   Heavens, no – I'm not anyone's dear papa.
I've no children at all.

Anuchkin   Oh, I'm sorry – I do beg your pardon.

Omelet (*aside*)   There's something suspicious about that
man's phizzog. I'll bet he's here for the same reason as
me. (*Aloud.*) No doubt you have some business with the
lady of the house?

Anuchkin   No, not really ... nothing in particular.
I've just dropped in on my way past.

Omelet (*aside*)   He's lying – on his way past, indeed!

It's a wife he's after, the scoundrel!

The doorbell rings. **Dunyashka** *rushes through the room to answer it. Voices off-stage: 'Is she at home?' 'Yes, sir, she is.'* **Zhevakin** *enters, accompanied by* **Dunyashka**.

Zhevakin (*to* **Dunyashka**)   Give me a bit of a brush down, my dear, if you don't mind. There's a fearful lot of dust on the streets, you know. And there's some fluff on there too, pick that off, please. (*Turns round.*) That's fine. Thank you, my dear. Look – isn't that a spider? Are you sure there's nothing on the flaps at the back? Thank you, my love. Mm . . . there's still something there, I think. (*He smoothes the sleeves of his frock-coat with his hand and looks at* **Anuchkin** *and* **Omelet**.) English cloth, you know. Lasts forever. Bought it in '95, when our squadron was in Sicily. I was still only a midshipman, had a uniform made out of it. Then in 1801, when Paul I was on the throne, I was made up to lieutenant, cloth was practically new. Went on a trip round the world in 1814, it started to get a little worn at the seams. Retired in 1815, had it turned inside-out, been wearing it the past ten years now, and it's as good as new still. Thank you, my dear . . . hmm . . . you're a sweet little thing! (*Kisses his hand to her, then goes up to the mirror and lightly ruffles his hair.*)

Anuchkin   If I may enquire, sir – you mentioned Sicily – is this Sicily a nice country?

Zhevakin   Wonderful! We spent thirty-four days there, and the scenery, I can tell you, is enchanting – those mountains, those little trees, some sort of pomegranate, yes, and the Italian girls, everywhere, they're such rosebuds, you just want to kiss them.

Anuchkin   And are they well educated?

Zhevakin   Oh, superbly! I tell you, only countesses here are as well educated. You'd walk down the street – well, a Russian lieutenant, of course, with epaulettes up here (*Points to his shoulders.*), and gold braid ... and they're such dark-eyed little beauties... Almost every house there, you know, has a little balcony, and the roofs are as flat as this floor. Anyway, you glance up, and there's one of these rosebuds sitting ... Well, of course, you don't want to look silly, so you ... (*Bows and waves.*) And she just does this ... (*Makes a slight movement with his hand.*) Naturally, she's dressed to kill: some sort of taffeta thing, like a corset, those earrings the ladies go in for ... in a word, a very tasty morsel.

Anuchkin   And if I may put another question to you, sir – what language do they use in Sicily?

Zhevakin   Oh, French, of course.

Anuchkin   And all the young ladies actually speak French?

Zhevakin   All of them, absolutely. Indeed, you may not believe, sir, what I am about to tell you, but we stayed there thirty-four days, and in all that time I never got a word of Russian out of them.

Anuchkin   Not one word?

Zhevakin   Not a one. I'm not talking about the nobility, and the other *signori* – their various officers, I mean – but you take the average peasant in those parts, dragging around all sorts of junk on his back, and you try saying in Russian: 'Give me some bread, friend,' well, I swear to God he won't understand you, but you say in French: '*Dateci del pane*', or '*Portate vino!*' he'll run right off and bring it.

Omelet   Well, the way I see it, it must be a strange place, this Sicily. Tell me – you mentioned a peasant just now ... what's this peasant like? Is he the same as a Russian peasant – broad-shouldered, ploughs the fields? Or doesn't he?

Zhevakin   I can't say. I didn't notice whether they

ploughed the fields or not, but I can tell you how they take snuff, yes – they don't just sniff it, they actually stuff it into their mouths. Transport's very cheap there too. The country's almost all water, and there are gondolas everywhere . . . naturally with one of these Italian girls, like a rosebud, sitting in them, with her little blouse, and her little headscarf. We had some English officers with us too – well, they were sailors, same as us, and at first it was very strange, we couldn't understand each other, but afterwards as we got better acquainted we got on famously – you'd point at a bottle or a glass, and they'd know right off that meant 'drink'. You'd put your fist up to your mouth, and go 'puff-puff' with your lips, and they'd know that meant 'smoke'. In fact, it's quite an easy language – after about three days the sailors could understand each other perfectly.

Omelet   You know, the way I see it, life in foreign lands is extremely interesting. And I'm delighted to make the acquaintance of a well-travelled man. Please, allow me to enquire with whom I have the honour of speaking?

Zhevakin   Zhevakin, sir – naval lieutenant, retired. On my part, may I also enquire with whom I have the honour of conversing?

Omelet   I'm an office manager by profession, sir – name's Omelet.

Zhevakin (*mishearing*)   Yes, I had a snack myself. Knew I had a fair long road ahead of me, and it's a bit chilly: managed a herring and a piece of bread.

Omelet   No, I think you've misheard me: that's my name – Omelet.

Zhevakin (*bowing*)   Oh, I beg your pardon, sir. I'm a little hard of hearing. I actually thought you were saying you'd eaten an omelette.

Omelet   I know, it can't be helped. I did think of

asking the general to let me change it to Omeletson, but the family talked me out of it. They said it'd be even worse.

Zhevakin Well, these things happen. Our entire third squadron, all the officers and men, they all had the queerest names, that's what our late commander Aleksei Ivanych used to say, he'd say that third squadron has some damn funny names – Slopsov, Tipsikov, Lieutenant Burntov. There was one midshipman, quite a good chap too – he was actually called Orifice. And the captain would shout: 'Hey you, Orifice, come over here!' He was forever making jokes about him. 'You're a right little Orifice,' he'd say.

The doorbell rings. **Fyokla** *hurries through the room to open the door.*

Omelet Good day to you, ma'am!

Zhevakin How are you, my dear?

Anuchkin Good morning, Madame Fyokla!

Fyokla (*in a great rush*) I'm fine, sirs, I'm fine, thank you!

She goes out to open the door, and voices are heard in the hall: 'Is she at home?' 'Yes, sir, she is'. Then a few barely audible words, to which **Fyokla** *responds with irritation: 'Who do you think you are!'* **Fyokla** *then re-enters with* **Kochkaryov** *and* **Podkolyosin**.

Kochkaryov (*to* **Podkolyosin**) Now remember – *courage,* that's the thing. (*Looks round, and bows, with some astonishment. Then, in an aside.*) Ye gods, what a crowd! What's the meaning of this? Surely they're not all after her? (*Nudges* **Fyokla** *and speaks in an undertone.*) Where'd you pick up these scarecrows, eh?

Fyokla (*sotto voce*) There's no scarecrows here, sir – they're all honest gentlemen.

Kochkaryov (*aside, to her*) 'Uninvited guests have well-darned vests.'

Fyokla Look at yourself, you've nothing to brag about. 'Your coat's cut from fine cloth, but you've no meat in your broth.'

Kochkaryov And what about these? 'Showing off their riches, with holes in their britches.' (*Aloud.*) Anyway, what is she doing now? I presume this is her bedroom door? (*Goes up to the door.*)

Fyokla Shame on you, sir – she's still getting dressed.

Kochkaryov So what harm am I doing? What's all the fuss? I'm just going to take a peek, that's all. (*Looks through the keyhole.*)

Zhevakin If you don't mind, sir – I'm curious too.

Omelet And me, please – just a little peep.

Kochkaryov (*still at the keyhole*) There's nothing to see, gentlemen. Some sort of white shape, you can't make out if it's a woman or a pillow . . . (*They all cluster round the door, trying to get a glimpse.*) Ssshh! Someone's coming . . . (*They spring back from the door.*)

Arina and **Agafya** *enter. All exchange bows.*

Arina Now, gentlemen, to what do we owe the pleasure of this visit?

Omelet Well, ma'am, I read in the papers that you wished to enter into a contract for the sale of some timber and firewood, and since I hold the position of manager in a government office, I've come to enquire as to what sort of timber, in what quantity, and how soon you can deliver it.

Arina Well, we're not actually in the timber business, but I'm pleased you've come nonetheless. What's your name, sir?

Omelet   Omelet, ma'am – that's Ivan Pavlovich, collegiate assessor.

Arina   Do sit down, please. (*Turns to* **Zhevakin**.) And if I might enquire, sir . . . ?

Zhevakin   I saw it in the paper too, some sort of advertisement, and I thought, well, I'll take a walk over – the weather looked set fair, and there's plenty of grass on the roads.

Arina   And your name, sir?

Zhevakin   Naval lieutenant, retired – name's Zhevakin. Baltazar Baltazarovich Zhevakin the Second. We had another Zhevakin, you see, but he retired before me. He was wounded, ma'am, just below the knee, and the bullet went right through him, oddly enough, didn't touch the knee-bone itself, but caught a tendon – threaded it like a needle, so if you were standing near him, it was as if he was trying to knee you in the behind.

Arina   Please, do have a seat. (*Turning to* **Anuchkin**.) And you, sir – may I enquire . . . ?

Anuchkin   Oh, a courtesy call, ma'am. Since I happen to be a fairly close neighbour . . .

Arina   Aren't you staying in Madame Tulubova's house, the merchant's widow, just opposite?

Anuchkin   No, I'm still living at the Sands, but I do intend moving to this end of town, and I'll be your neighbour eventually.

Arina   Please sit down. (*Turning to* **Kochkaryov**.) Now, sir, if I might enquire . . . ?

Kochkaryov   You mean to say you don't recognise me? (*Turns to* **Agafya**.) And you too, dear lady?

Agafya   As far as I know, I've never seen you before.

Kochkaryov Well, anyway, try to remember. You must have seen me somewhere.

Agafya I honestly don't recall. It wasn't at the Biryushkins', was it?

Kochkaryov The Biryushkins' – it was indeed.

Agafya Oh dear, you haven't heard about her terrible misfortune?

Kochkaryov Yes, she got married, of course.

Agafya No no, that would be wonderful. No, she broke her leg.

Arina Broke it quite badly, too. She was coming home late one night in a cab, and the driver was drunk, and tipped her out.

Kochkaryov That's right – I remember there was something. Either she got married or broke her leg.

Arina And what's your name, sir?

Kochkaryov Why, it's Kochkaryov, of course. – Ilya Fomich – we're practically cousins. My wife's always saying how . . . oh, excuse me . . . (*Takes* **Podkolyosin** *by the hand and leads him up.*) Permit me to introduce my good friend Podkolyosin – Ivan Kuzmich – he's a court councillor, he's in the service as a despatcher, but he does all the business himself, he's brought his department to an absolute pitch of perfection.

Arina And what's his name?

Kochkaryov Podkolyosin – Ivan Kuzmich Podkolyosin. There's a head of department just for show, but he does all the work. Ivan Kuzmich Podkolyosin.

Arina Really? Now, please be seated, gentlemen.

Enter **Starikov**. *He bows to the company briskly and rapidly, like a shopkeeper, his hands resting lightly on his sides.*

Starikov (*to* **Arina**) Good morning, dear lady. The lads at the bazaar were saying you had some wool to sell, ma'am, is that so?

Agafya *turns her back on him disdainfully, and speaks under her breath, but so that he can hear.*

Agafya This isn't a shop!

Starikov Eh? Have we come at a bad time? Or have you struck a deal without us?

Arina Mr Starikov, come in, please do. We've no wool to sell, but we're happy to see you. Please be seated.

All are now seated. A silence.

Omelet Strange weather we're having. Looked quite like rain this morning, but it seems to have passed over now.

Agafya Indeed, sir, I've never seen anything like it: one minute it's bright, next minute it's pouring. It's extremely disagreeable.

Zhevakin Now, in Sicily, dear lady – we were there with our squadron in the spring, but if you reckon it out, it was actually our February – anyway, you'd step outside and it'd be a sunny day, and next thing you'd feel a spot of rain, you'd look up, and sure enough, here it comes.

Omelet The worst thing in this kind of weather is to be stuck on your own. It's different altogether for a married man, he's never bored, but if you're on your own, it's just . . .

Zhevakin Oh, it's deadly, just deadly.

Anuchkin Yes, you can say that again.

Kochkaryov Yes, indeed, it's absolute torture. You wish you were dead. God preserve us from such a fate, eh?

Omelet Anyway, ma'am – supposing you had to choose an object of your affections? What would be to your taste, might I ask? You'll forgive my being so direct, but which branch of the service do you consider most fitting for a husband?

Zhevakin Wouldn't you prefer, dear lady, a husband well acquainted with the stormy seas?

Kochkaryov No no no – the best husband, in my opinion, is the man who can run a whole department practically single-handed.

Anuchkin Now, let's not prejudge the matter. Surely you wouldn't despise a man who, although he's served in the infantry, of course, nevertheless knows how to appreciate the finer points of polite society?

Omelet Will you decide, ma'am?

Agafya *is silent.*

Fyokla Do answer, my dear. Say something.

Omelet What's it to be, dear lady?

Kochkaryov What's your view on the matter? Miss Agafya?

Fyokla (*aside to her*) Do say something – say 'Thank you', or 'It's my pleasure'. It's not nice, just sitting there.

Agafya (*sotto voce*) I'm embarrassed, I'm just so embarrassed – I'm leaving, Auntie, I really am – you stay behind.

Fyokla No, don't do that, don't go, you'll disgrace yourself. Heaven knows what they'll think.

Agafya (*sotto voce*) No, I'm leaving, I've got to, I really must!

Rushes out, followed by **Fyokla** *and* **Arina**.

Omelet   Well, I never – they've all cleared off. What's going on?

Kochkaryov   Must be some sort of accident.

Zhevakin   Something to do with the lady's dress – needing fixed, or whatever . . . maybe a pin in her blouse.

Fyokla *enters. All go to meet her with questions: 'What is it? What's the matter?'*

Kochkaryov   Is something wrong?

Fyokla   Good heavens, how could anything be wrong? No, no, not at all.

Kochkaryov   Well, why did she leave, then?

Fyokla   You made her feel embarrassed, that's why she went out. You put her in such a muddle she couldn't sit still. Anyway, she asks you to excuse her, and to come for a cup of tea this evening. (*Exits.*)

Omelet (*aside*)   Huh! I know these cups of tea. That's what I don't like about this matchmaking business, it's such a carry-on. They can't say today, but come back tomorrow, and then again for tea the next day, and they still need time to consider. It's a load of rubbish, really, not worth racking your brains over – oh, to hell with it, I'm a busy man, I've no time for this.

Kochkaryov (*to* **Podkolyosin**)   The young lady's not bad-looking, though.

Podkolyosin   Mm, not bad.

Zhevakin   She's actually quite pretty.

Kochkaryov (*aside*)   Damn! The old fool's fallen for her. He might get in the way. (*Aloud.*) No, not pretty. Definitely not pretty.

Omelet   Her nose is too big.

Zhevakin No, surely not. I didn't even notice her nose. She's such a little rosebud.

Anuchkin I agree with them – she's not quite the thing, not really. I even doubt if she's acquainted with the finer points of polite society. And does she know French, besides?

Zhevakin Well, if I may be so bold, sir – why didn't you test her? Why didn't you speak French with her? Maybe she does know it.

Anuchkin What, d'you think I can speak French? No, I've not had the good fortune to enjoy that sort of education. My father was a scoundrel, sir, a brute. He never even dreamed of teaching me French. And it would've been easy then, when I was still a child. All he'd to do was give me a sound whipping, I'd have spoken French all right, indeed I would.

Zhevakin Yes, but you don't speak it now, so what good would it do you if she . . .

Anuchkin No no, a woman's an entirely different matter. She absolutely must speak French. Without it, her . . . um, what d'you call it . . . (*Points and gesticulates.*) No, she'll never be quite right.

Omelet (*aside*) Well, I'll let them worry about that. Meanwhile I'll go and inspect the house and extensions from outside, and if it's all up to scratch, I'll settle the business this very evening. I've nothing to fear from these fellows – wishy-washy creatures the lot of them. Ladies don't care for that type. (*Exits.*)

Zhevakin Well, I'm going for a smoke. Incidentally, don't we go the same way? Where do you live, may I ask?

Anuchkin The Sands, in Petrov Lane.

Zhevakin Mm, it's a little out of my road. I live on the island, the Eighteenth Row, but I'll keep you company anyway. (*They exit.*)

Starikov   No, this is too rich for my blood. Well, you'll come round to me eventually, Miss Agafya. My respects, gentlemen. (*Bows and exits.*)

Podkolyosin   Come on, we'll go too.

Kochkaryov   But the young lady is rather sweet, isn't she?

Podkolyosin   You think so? I don't like her, frankly.

Kochkaryov   Eh? Since when? You said yourself she was pretty.

Podkolyosin   No no, there's something not right. Her nose is too big, and she can't speak French.

Kochkaryov   So what? What d'you want French for?

Podkolyosin   A young lady ought to speak French, really.

Kochkaryov   What on earth for?

Podkolyosin   Well, because ... oh, I don't know, but she'll never be quite right without it.

Kochkaryov   You see? Some fool's just said that and he's taken it in. She's a peach, an absolute peach. You won't find a girl like that anywhere.

Podkolyosin   All right, she did catch my eye at first, but afterwards when they started going on about her long nose, well, I had a good look, and I could see for myself, she had a long nose.

Kochkaryov   Oh you, you couldn't see a barn door in front of you. They were saying that on purpose, to put you off. And I wasn't singing her praises either, that's how these things are done. I tell you, my friend, this is some girl! You just look at her eyes – ye gods, what eyes she has! They speak, they practically breathe! And that nose? Well, what can you say about her nose? Pure white – like alabaster! And not just any old sort of alabaster, either. Have a close look at it yourself.

Podkolyosin (*smiling*)   Yes, I can see now, she might be quite pretty.

Kochkaryov   Why, of course she's pretty! Listen, now that they've all gone, let's go in and propose, and get everything settled.

Podkolyosin   Oh no, I couldn't do that.

Kochkaryov   Why not?

Podkolyosin   Well, it's a bit cheeky. There's so many of us. She should take her pick.

Kochkaryov   Why are you bothering about them? Afraid of the competition, is that it? I'll send the whole lot packing in a minute, if you like.

Podkolyosin   And how exactly will you do that?

Kochkaryov   You leave that to me. Just promise me you won't back out later.

Podkolyosin   Yes, why not? Go ahead, I've no objections. I do want to get married.

Kochkaryov   Your hand on it, sir!

Podkolyosin (*giving him his hand*)   Right!

Kochkaryov   Now, that's all I need. (*Both exit.*)

Curtain.

Act Two

The same room in **Agafya**'s *house.*

Agafya (*alone*) Honestly, this choosing business is so difficult. If there were just one or two, but four! Take your pick. Mr Anuchkin isn't bad-looking, but he's a bit skinny, of course. And Mr Podkolyosin isn't too bad, either. And truth to tell, though he's rather stout, Mr Omelet's still a fine figure of a man. So what am I to do, if you please? Mr Zhevakin's also a man of distinction. It really is difficult to decide, you can't begin to describe it. Now, if you could attach Mr Anuchkin's lips to Mr Podkolyosin's nose, and take some of Mr Zhevakin's easy manner, and perhaps add Mr Omelet's solid build, I could decide on the spot. But now I've got to rack my brains! And it's giving me a fearsome headache. I think it'd be best to draw lots. Turn the whole matter over to God's will, and whichever one comes out, that'll be my husband. I'll write all their names on bits of paper, roll them up tight, then so be it. (*She goes over to her desk, takes out scissors and paper, cuts it up into slips, writes on them, and rolls them up, still talking.*) Life's so trying for a girl, especially when she's in love. It's something no man will ever understand, and anyway they just don't want to. Now, that's them ready! All that remains is to put them in my purse, shut my eyes, and that's it — what will be, will be. (*Puts the slips of paper into her purse and gives it a shake.*) This is dreadful ... oh God, please make it Mr Anuchkin! No, why him? Better Mr Podkolyosin. But why Mr Podkolyosin? In what way are the others worse? No, no, I won't ... whichever comes out, so be it. (*She rummages in her purse and pulls them all out instead of one.*) Oh! All of them! They've all come out! And my heart's pounding. No, no, it's got to be one!

Puts the slips back in her purse and mixes them. At that moment, **Kochkaryov** *stealthily enters and stands behind her.*

Agafya   Oh, if only I could draw out Baltazar ... no, what am I saying? I mean Mr Anuchkin ... no, I won't, I won't. Let fate decide.

Kochkaryov   Take Podkolyosin – he's the best of the bunch.

Agafya   Oh! (*Shrieks and covers her face with her hands, afraid to look behind her.*)

Kochkaryov   What are you frightened of? Don't be alarmed, it's only me. Honestly, you should take Podkolyosin.

Agafya   Oh, I'm so ashamed – you overheard.

Kochkaryov   Oh, never mind – I mean, I'm family, we're related. There's no need to be embarrassed in front of me. Now, take your hands away from that pretty face of yours.

Agafya   (*half-uncovers her face*)   I really am ashamed.

Kochkaryov   Anyway, do – take Podkolyosin.

Agafya   Oh! (*Shrieks and covers her face again.*)

Kochkaryov   Seriously, he's a wonderful man – he's licked that office of his into shape, he's an absolute marvel.

Agafya   (*gradually uncovering her face*)   Yes, but what about the others? I mean, Mr Anuchkin – he's a fine man too.

Kochkaryov   Oh, please – he's rubbish beside Podkolyosin.

Agafya   Why's that?

Kochkaryov   Well, it's obvious. Podkolyosin's a man who ... well, he's the sort of man ... you won't find his like anywhere.

Agafya   And what about Mr Omelet?

Kochkaryov   He's rubbish too, they're all rubbish.

Agafya   Surely not all of them?

Kochkaryov   Well, judge for yourself, you've only got to compare them. It's Podkolyosin on every count, no matter what. And these Anuchkins, these Omelets, God knows what they are.

Agafya   But they seem quite . . . well, mannerly, really.

Kochkaryov   Mannerly? They're louts, the very worst sort of bullies. Of course, if you want to be beaten up the day after your wedding . . .

Agafya   Oh, my God! That's dreadful, there couldn't be anything worse.

Kochkaryov   No, indeed. That's the worst thing you could imagine.

Agafya   So you would advise me to take Mr Podkolyosin?

Kochkaryov   Podkolyosin, yes, of course Podkolyosin. (*Aside.*) I think this is working. Podkolyosin's waiting in the cake-shop, I'd better run and get him.

Agafya   So, you think Mr Podkolyosin?

Kochkaryov   Podkolyosin – absolutely.

Agafya   And the others – should I really refuse them?

Kochkaryov   Yes, of course.

Agafya   But how can I do that? I mean, it's a bit embarrassing.

Kochkaryov   Why? Just tell them you're too young, you don't want to get married.

Agafya   But they won't believe it, will they. They'll start asking why.

Kochkaryov   Look, if you want to be done with it once and for all, just say, 'Clear off, you idiots!'

Agafya   Oh, I couldn't say that, could I?

Kochkaryov   You give it a try. They'll make a quick getaway after that, I assure you.

Agafya   But wouldn't that be a bit rude?

Kochkaryov   So? You won't be seeing them again, so who cares?

Agafya   Just the same, it isn't very nice. They'll be angry.

Kochkaryov   So what if they are angry? If anything could come of it, it'd be a different matter, but the worst that can happen is if one of them spits in your eye, that's all.

Agafya   There, you see!

Kochkaryov   So where's the harm in that? Ye gods, some people have been spat at more than once. One fellow I know – terribly handsome, rosy cheeks and all – he kept on pestering his boss for a raise, till he finally couldn't stand it – spat right in his face, I swear to God! 'There you are,' he says, 'there's your raise! Now clear off, you son of Satan!' But he gave him a raise just the same. So what if they do spit? It'd be different if you'd no handkerchief, but you've got one right there in your pocket. Take it out and wipe it off. (*The doorbell rings.*) That'll be one of them at the door, I'd rather not see them just now. There isn't another way out, by any chance?

Agafya   Yes, of course, by the back stairs. But honestly, I'm trembling all over.

Kochkaryov   Don't worry. Presence of mind, that's the thing. Goodbye! (*Aside.*) I'll hurry and get Podkolyoskin. (*Exits.*)

Omelet *enters.*

Omelet   I've come a little early on purpose, ma'am, to

have a word with you in private, and at leisure.
Anyway, ma'am, concerning my rank, I assume you're
aware that I am a collegiate assessor, well liked by my
superiors, and obeyed by my subordinates ... the only
thing I lack is a partner to share my life.

Agafya Ah, yes.

Omelet And now I have found my partner in life.
That partner is you, ma'am. Tell me straight out: yes or
no? (*Stares at her shoulders. Aside.*) Hm, she's not one of
these skinny German women – there's a bit of flesh on
her.

Agafya I'm still quite young, sir. I'm not disposed to
marry yet ...

Omelet Well, for goodness' sake, what's the
matchmaker doing here? Perhaps you mean something
else ... explain, please. (*The bell rings.*) Damn! Just when
I was getting down to business!

Zhevakin *enters.*

Zhevakin I beg your pardon, ma'am – perhaps I'm a
little early. (*Turns and sees* **Omelet**.) Ah, there's someone
already here ... my respects, dear sir.

Omelet (*aside*) Damn you and your respects! (*Aloud.*)
Anyway, ma'am – what is it to be? In one word – yes,
or no? (*The bell rings again.* **Omelet** *is in a spitting rage.*)
That bell again!

Anuchkin *enters.*

Anuchkin Ma'am, I'm perhaps a little earlier than the
rules of propriety would dictate ... (*Seeing the other two,
utters an exclamation and bows.*) My respects, gentlemen.

Omelet (*aside*) You keep your respects to yourself!
Who the hell invited you anyway? Pity you didn't break
those damn spindly legs of yours! (*Aloud.*) Now, ma'am,
make up your mind – I'm a busy man, I've no time to

spare: yes or no?

Agafya (*in confusion*) Sir, that's enough ... Please, that's enough ... (*Aside.*) I don't know what I'm saying.

Omelet What d'you mean, enough? In what way enough?

Agafya Nothing, sir, nothing ... I didn't mean ... (*Plucking up courage.*) Oh, clear off! (*Aside, clasping her hands.*) Heavens, what've I said?

Omelet What? Clear off? What's that supposed to mean? Clear off! Permit me to enquire, ma'am, what you intend by that? (*Hands on hips, he advances menacingly towards her.*)

Agafya (*takes one look at him and shrieks*) Oh! He's going to hit me! He's going to hit me!

She runs out. **Omelet** *remains, standing open-mouthed. Hearing the shriek,* **Arina** *rushes in, and at the sight of* **Omelet**'s *face, she too cries out: 'Oh! He's going to hit us!' Exits.*

Omelet Well, I'm be damned. What a carry-on!

The doorbell rings, and voices are heard.

Kochkaryov (*off-stage*) Go on, go on, what are you stopping for?

Podkolyosin (*off-stage*) No, you go first. I need a minute to tidy myself up, my boot-strap's undone.

Kochkaryov (*off-stage*) Yes, and you'll sneak off again.

Podkolyosin (*off-stage*) No, I won't. I won't, I swear!

Kochkaryov (*entering*) That's all I need – him and his confounded boot-strap!

Omelet (*to* **Kochkaryov**) Tell me, sir – is this young lady crazy or what?

Kochkaryov Why? Has something happened?

Omelet Oh yes – quite irrational behaviour. Ran out of the room, started screaming: 'He's going to hit me! He's going to hit me!' I'm damned if I know what it's about.

Kochkaryov Ah well, she does take the odd turn. She's a bit touched.

Omelet So tell me – you're a relative of hers, aren't you?

Kochkaryov Indeed I am, sir.

Omelet What sort of relative, if I might enquire?

Kochkaryov I honestly don't know, sir. My mother's aunt is something or other to her father, or else her father is something to my aunt – my wife knows, that's her territory.

Omelet And she has been having these turns for a while?

Kochkaryov Since childhood, sir.

Omelet Hm. Well, it'd be better if she had some brains, but I don't mind if she's a bit simple. As long as the marriage settlement's in order.

Kochkaryov You know she has absolutely nothing?

Omelet Eh? What about the stone house?

Kochkaryov That? That's just talk. I mean, if you knew how it was built . . . The walls are just one course of brick, and there's all kinds of junk behind it, rubble, woodchips, sawdust . . .

Omelet You're not serious?

Kochkaryov Indeed I am, sir. That's how they build houses these days, didn't you know? Anything they can get a mortgage on.

Omelet But the house isn't mortgaged, surely?

Kochkaryov   Who told you that? The fact is, it's not only mortgaged, they haven't paid the interest for the past two years. And there's a brother in the Senate – he's got his eye on the property, you couldn't imagine a more devious, grasping individual. He'd sell the clothes off his own mother's back, the godless wretch.

Omelet   So how come that old matchmaker . . . Why, the monster, she's a beast in human . . . (*Aside.*) But maybe *he's* lying. By God, I'll put that old creature to the test! And if he's telling the truth, well . . . I'll make her sing out of the wrong side of her mouth!

Anuchkin   Sir, if I might also trouble you with an enquiry? I must confess that, not knowing French myself, I find it extremely difficult to judge whether a woman can speak French or not. Now, this young lady . . .

Kochkaryov   Not a word.

Anuchkin   Eh?

Kochkaryov   Not a syllable. I know that for a fact. She went to the same boarding school as my wife, and she was notoriously lazy, never out of the dunce's cap. The French teacher used to beat her with a stick.

Anuchkin   Fancy that! You know, from the minute I clapped eyes on her I had a feeling she didn't know French.

Omelet   Oh, to hell with French! But as for that damned matchmaker . . . what a beast! Damned old witch! I mean, you wouldn't believe how she laid it on – a work of art, an absolute picture! 'A house,' she says, 'with an extension, stone foundations, silver spoons, a sleigh – just hop in and drive off . . .' I tell you, you wouldn't find a better description in a novel! The old bag! Just wait till I get my hands on . . . Aha! Here she is!

Fyokla *enters.*

Omelet   Right, you just come over here, you old sinner! Come here!

Anuchkin   So this is how you've deceived me, Madame Fyokla.

Kochkaryov   Come on, step up and face the music, you wicked woman!

Fyokla   I can't make out a word – you're deafening me.

Omelet   One course of brick, you old trollop! And you told me it had a mezzanine and God knows what else!

Fyokla   Well, I don't know – it wasn't me that built it. Maybe it only needed one course of brick, maybe that's how they built it.

Omelet   Yes, and it's mortgaged into the bargain! Damn you, I hope you roast in hell, you old witch! (*Stamping his foot.*)

Fyokla   Heavens, would you listen to this! And swearing too. Anybody else would be thanking me for all the trouble I went to.

Anuchkin   Yes, and you told me that she knew French.

Fyokla   Indeed she does, my dear sir – and German, and all the rest. Whatever accomplishments you want, she's got them all.

Anuchkin   Oh, no no – apparently she can only speak Russian.

Fyokla   So where's the harm in that? Russian's easier to understand, that's why she speaks it. And if she could speak some heathen tongue, what good would that do? You wouldn't understand a word of it. I surely don't have to tell you what Russian is, everybody knows that – all the blessed saints spoke Russian.

Omelet   Right, you just come over here, damn you!

Fyokla (*backing away towards the door*)   No, indeed I won't
– I know what you're like. You're a hard man, you hit
folk for no reason!

Omelet   Well, you watch out, dearie, you won't get
away with this. I'll run you down to the police, you'll
find out what it means to cheat honest people! Yes,
you'll see. And you can tell that young woman she's a
fraud! D'you hear? An absolute fraud! (*Exits.*)

Fyokla   Well, how about that, eh? Flew right off the
handle! And because he's fat, he thinks nobody's a
match for him. Well, I'm telling you you're a fraud
yourself, so there!

Anuchkin   Actually, dear lady, I must confess I didn't
think you'd deceive me in this way. If I'd known what
sort of education she'd had, well . . . I'd never have set
foot in the house. Indeed no, ma'am. (*Exits.*)

Fyokla   They've either gone crazy, or else they've been
at the bottle. Honestly, what a bunch of nit-pickers! It's
all that silly book-learning, it's addled their brains!

Kochkaryov *roars with laughter, looking at* **Fyokla**, *and
pointing his finger at her.*

Fyokla (*annoyed*)   What are you guffawing about?
(**Kochkaryov** *goes on laughing.*) Is he having a seizure?

Kochkaryov   Well, some matchmaker you are!
Matchmaker, indeed! Madame the marriage-broker, she
can fix everything! (*Goes on laughing.*)

Fyokla   Just listen to him sniggering! My God, your
mother must've been off her head when she had you!
(*Exits in high dudgeon.*)

Kochkaryov (*still laughing*)   Oh, I can't, I can't take
any more, I'll split my sides, I'm going to burst!

Zhevakin *looks at him, begins laughing too.* **Kochkaryov**

sinks into a chair, exhausted.

Kochkaryov   Oh God, I'm worn out. If I laugh any more I'll burst a blood vessel.

Zhevakin   You know, I do like your cheerful disposition, sir. We had a young midshipman in Captain Boldyrev's squadron – name of Petukhov, Anton Ivanovich – and he had a very similar disposition. At times you could show him a finger, that's all it took, and he'd burst out laughing, I swear to God – and he'd be laughing the whole day. And sometimes you'd look at him, and it'd be so funny, you'd end up laughing yourself.

Kochkaryov   (*recovering his breath*)   Oh, Lord have mercy on us sinners! What on earth was the silly woman thinking of? Her, make a match? Huh! Now, when I fix 'em up, I do a proper job.

Zhevakin   Seriously? Can you really arrange a marriage?

Kochkaryov   Absolutely. Anybody to anybody, whoever you like.

Zhevakin   Well, if that's true – marry me to this young lady here.

Kochkaryov   You? What do you want to get married for?

Zhevakin   What d'you mean, what for? That's a rather strange question, if you don't mind my saying. It's obvious what for.

Kochkaryov   But you've just heard she has no dowry.

Zhevakin   Well, if that's the case, so be it. It's too bad, of course, but she's a extremely charming girl, terribly well-mannered – one might get along quite well without a dowry. A comfortable little room . . . (*Indicates the size with his hands.*) with a small ante-room, a little screen, or something like this partition . . .

Kochkaryov Yes, but what is it you actually like about her?

Zhevakin Well, to tell you the truth, I like her because she's plump. I'm something of a connoisseur of female plumpness.

Kochkaryov (*with a sidelong glance at him, speaks aside*) He's not exactly a fashion-plate himself. He looks like a pouch with the tobacco shaken out. (*Aloud.*) No, you shouldn't get married.

Zhevakin How's that?

Kochkaryov Well, strictly between ourselves, you don't cut much of a figure, do you? Chicken legs . . .

Zhevakin Chicken legs?

Kochkaryov That's right. I mean, what do you look like?

Zhevakin What are you talking about – chicken legs?

Kochkaryov Just what I say – chicken legs.

Zhevakin Sir, that strikes me as being a rather personal remark . . .

Kochkaryov Look, I'm only telling you this because I know you're a sensible person. I wouldn't say it to anyone else. I'll fix you up if you like, but to some other lady.

Zhevakin No, no, I beg you – don't fix me up with anyone else. Be so kind as to make it this one.

Kochkaryov All right, I'll do it, but on one condition: that you don't interfere in any way, or even let the young lady set eyes on you. I'll arrange it all without you.

Zhevakin But how can you do all that without me? I mean, I'll have to put in an appearance, surely?

Kochkaryov That won't be necessary. Just go home and wait – it'll all be fixed up by this evening.

Zhevakin (*rubbing his hands*) Well, that would be splendid! But won't you need my diploma, my service record? The young lady might wish to make enquiries. I can run home, it'll only take a minute to get them.

Kochkaryov You don't need anything, just go home. I'll let you know this very day. (*Ushers him out.*) Huh! In a pig's ear I'll let you know! Now, what's going on? What's keeping Podkolyosin? It's most peculiar. He can't still be fixing his boot-strap. I'd better nip out and fetch him.

Agafya *enters.*

Agafya (*looking round*) Well, have they gone? There's no one here?

Kochkaryov Yes, yes, they've gone.

Agafya Oh, if you only knew how I was trembling all over! I've never been so scared. That Omelet creature's really terrifying, he'd be a fearful tyrant to his wife. I keep thinking he'll be back any minute.

Kochkaryov No, he won't be back. I'll stake my life on it, neither of those two'll poke his nose in here again.

Agafya And what about the other one?

Kochkaryov What other one?

Zhevakin (*popping his head round the door*) Oh, I'm just dying to hear how she'll declare her love for me with that pretty little mouth of hers . . . an absolute rosebud!

Agafya Mr Zhevakin?

Zhevakin That's it! Here it comes! (*Rubbing his hands.*)

Kochkaryov Him? Oh, to hell with him. I couldn't imagine who you were talking about. No, he's out of the question, an utter buffoon.

Zhevakin What's this all about? I must say, I don't understand.

Agafya I thought he looked like quite a nice man.

Kochkaryov A drunkard!

Zhevakin What on earth's going on?

Agafya He's not a drunkard, is he?

Kochkaryov And out-and-out scoundrel, ma'am, believe me.

Zhevakin (*aloud*) No, excuse me, sir – that's not what I asked you to say! Something in my favour, a word of praise – that's another matter entirely – but if you're going on like that, using that sort of language, well, I'd rather have somebody else, and much obliged to you, sir!

Kochkaryov (*aside*) What possessed him to turn up? (*To* **Agafya**, *sotto voce*.) Look, look at him, he can barely stand up! He's staggering all over the place. Kick him out, and be done with him! (*Aside*.) And Podkolyosin's still not here! Damned scoundrel! I'll get my own back on him! (*Exits*.)

Zhevakin (*aside*) He promised he'd speak up for me, and instead of that he's been abusing me! What a strange creature! (*Aloud*.) Ma'am, you mustn't believe . . .

Agafya Excuse me, I don't feel very well . . . I have a headache. (*Makes to exit*.)

Zhevakin But perhaps there *is* something about me you don't like? (*Points to his head*.) It's not my little bald spot, is it? You mustn't mind that, that's nothing, I got it from a fever, it'll grow in again in no time.

Agafya Sir, I don't care what you have up there.

Zhevakin And when I'm wearing a black coat, ma'am, my complexion does look a bit lighter.

Agafya That's good, I'm pleased for you. Now, goodbye! (*Exits.*)

Zhevakin (*calling after her*) Ma'am, please! Tell me the reason. Why? What for? Is it some fundamental flaw, or what? ... She's gone! Now, that's most peculiar! I mean, that must be the seventeenth time that's happened to me, and it's almost always the same thing. At first everything seems to be going smoothly, then when it comes to the bit ... well, they turn me down. (*Paces around the room, deep in thought.*) Yes ... this is actually the seventeenth. And what on earth does she want? What is she expecting, for instance, in the way of ... What reason ... ? (*After some thought.*) No, it's a mystery, a complete mystery. I could understand it if I were ugly or something. (*Looks himself over.*) But I don't think anyone could say that. No, everything's as it should be, thank God. Nature hasn't been unkind to me. I just can't fathom it. Maybe I should go home and search through my trunk – I used to have a poem, no woman could resist it. Honestly, this passes belief. At first you think your luck's in ... Oh well, I obviously have to start from scratch again. It's such a pity, it really is. (*Exits.*)

Podkolyosin *and* **Kochkaryov** *enter, and both look behind them.*

Kochkaryov He didn't spot us! Did you see the long face he was wearing?

Podkolyosin D'you mean to say he's been refused too?

Kochkaryov Point blank.

Podkolyosin (*with a smug smile*) Must be pretty upsetting, though, to be turned down.

Kochkaryov Extremely!

Podkolyosin Even so, I still can't believe she told you straight out that she prefers me to all the others.

Kochkaryov   Prefers, nothing! She's absolutely mad about you. Such love! The pet names she calls you, such passion! She's besotted with you, I tell you.

Podkolyosin (*smirking*)   Well, women do say all sorts of things when they feel like it – things you'd never imagine: chubby-cheeks, my little cockroach, my little black spider . . .

Kochkaryov   And that's nothing. You wait till you've been married a couple of months, you'll hear plenty of names then. You'll simply melt away, my friend.

Podkolyosin (*simpers*)   Really?

Kochkaryov   On my honour, sir. Now listen, we've got to work quickly. Declare your love for her, open your heart, and ask for her hand this very minute.

Podkolyosin   This minute? What are you talking about?

Kochkaryov   It's got to be right now . . . look, here she comes.

Agafya *enters.*

Kochkaryov   Ma'am, I've brought you this mortal creature whom you behold. Never has any man been so much in love. Indeed, God forbid that even my worst enemy should . . .

Podkolyosin (*nudging him in the ribs, aside*)   You're laying it on a bit thick, old man.

Kochkaryov (*aside, to him*)   Don't worry, it's all right. (*To her, sotto voce.*) You'll have to be more forceful, he's terribly shy. Try and be a little more relaxed. Flutter your eyelashes at him, or lower your eyes, then give him both barrels, the villain. Flash him a bit of shoulder, let the wretch have a look! It's a pity you're not wearing a dress with short sleeves, but this'll do well enough. (*Aloud.*) So, I shall leave you in pleasant company, ma'am. I'll just pop into your dining-room and kitchen for a minute. I've some things to attend to. The caterer I ordered supper from will be here soon, and the wine might have arrived . . . *Au revoir!* (*To* **Podkolyosin**.) Now, go to it, man! (*Exits.*)

Agafya Please be seated.

They sit down and remain silent.

Podkolyosin Do you like boating, ma'am?

Agafya Boating?

Podkolyosin It's very pleasant, boating in the summer.

Agafya Well, yes, I go on the occasional trip with friends.

Podkolyosin There's no telling what kind of summer we'll have, though.

Agafya I do hope it'll be fine.

They fall silent.

Podkolyosin What kind of flower do you like best, ma'am?

Agafya Oh, anything with a strong scent – carnations, I think.

Podkolyosin Flowers are just the thing for ladies.

Agafya Yes, it's a pleasant pastime. (*A silence.*) Which church did you attend last Sunday?

Podkolyosin The Church of the Ascension, ma'am. But the week before I was at the Kazan Cathedral. Doesn't matter which church you go to, you can pray just the same, but the decorations are nicer in the cathedral.

They fall silent. **Podkolyosin** *begins drumming his fingers on the table.*

It'll soon be festival time again, at Yekaterinhof.

Agafya   Yes, in another month, I think.

Podkolyosin   Not even a month.

Agafya   I expect it'll be quite jolly.

Podkolyosin   Today's the eighth . . . (*Counting on his fingers.*) That's the ninth, tenth, eleventh . . . yes, twenty-two days to go.

Agafya   Fancy, so soon!

Podkolyosin   Not counting today, of course. (*A silence.*) Yes, the Russians are such a brave people!

Agafya   I'm sorry?

Podkolyosin   I mean the workers. They stand right at the very top . . . I was walking past a house, and there was a plasterer at work, and he wasn't in the least afraid.

Agafya   Really? Where was that?

Podkolyosin   On the road I take into the office every day. You know I go into my department every morning.

A silence. **Podkolyosin** *begins drumming his fingers again. Finally he picks up his hat and bows.*

Agafya   Surely you're not . . . ?

Podkolyosin   Yes, ma'am, I must. I'm sorry if I've been boring you.

Agafya   Oh no, never! On the contrary, I should thank you for helping me to pass the time so agreeably.

Podkolyosin (*smiling*)   I honestly thought I was boring you.

Agafya   No, not at all, sir.

Podkolyosin   Well, if that's the case, perhaps you'll allow me to call some other time, in the evening . . .

Agafya   I'd be delighted, sir.

They bow. **Podkolyosin** *exits.*

Agafya (*alone*)   What a fine upstanding man! It's only
now I've got to know him, and truly, one can't help
loving him, he's so modest and sensible. Yes indeed, his
friend spoke the truth. It's just a pity he's left so soon,
I'd have enjoyed listening to him some more, it's a joy
to talk with him! What's especially nice is that he's not
one for idle chatter. I'd have liked to say a few things
myself, but I must confess I felt terribly shy, my heart
was starting to pound so . . . Yes, he's a first-rate man!
I'll go and tell Auntie . . . (*Exits.*)

Podkolyosin *and* **Kochkaryov** *enter.*

Kochkaryov   What are you going home for? What
nonsense is this? Why are you going home?

Podkolyosin   But what's the point of staying here?
I've said all I needed to.

Kochkaryov   What, you've opened your heart to her?

Podkolyosin   Well, no, not exactly. I haven't opened
it yet.

Kochkaryov   Damn it to hell, man, why didn't you?

Podkolyosin   What, you want me to come right out
with it, before I've talked about anything else? Just out
of the blue: 'Please, miss, will you marry me?'

Kochkaryov   Well, for God's sake, what rubbish *have*
you been talking the past half-hour?

Podkolyosin   We chatted about all sorts of things.
And I was well pleased, let me tell you. We passed the
time extremely agreeably.

Kochkaryov   Listen, when are we going to sort all this
out? I mean, we're supposed to be at the church in an
hour, for the wedding!

Podkolyosin Good God, are you mad? The wedding today!

Kochkaryov Why ever not?

Podkolyosin Today!

Kochkaryov But you gave your word. You said you'd marry her as soon as we'd got rid of the other suitors.

Podkolyosin Well, I'm not going back on my word, only not right now – I need at least a month's breathing space.

Kochkaryov A month!

Podkolyosin Yes, of course.

Kochkaryov Are you crazy?

Podkolyosin I can't do it in less.

Kochkaryov But I've already ordered the supper from the caterer, you idiot! Listen, Ivan Kuzmich, dear friend . . . don't be stubborn, get married now.

Podkolyosin What? What are you saying? What do you mean, now?

Kochkaryov Ivan Kuzmich, please! If you won't do it for your own sake, then at least do it for mine.

Podkolyosin Honestly, I can't.

Kochkaryov Yes, you can, dear friend, you can. Now, don't be naughty . . . *please?*

Podkolyosin No, I can't, honestly – it's such an awkward business.

Kochkaryov What d'you mean, awkward? Who told you it was awkward? Think for yourself for once. You're an intelligent man, right? I'm not saying that to flatter you, not just because you're a despatcher, I'm saying it out of affection. Now, come on, my dear friend, make your mind up. Try and see things like a rational person.

Podkolyosin Oh, if only that were possible, I'd . . .

Kochkaryov Ivan Kuzmich! Sweetheart! Angel! Do you want me to go down on my knees?

Podkolyosin What on earth for?

Kochkaryov (*goes down on his knees*) There! I'm on my knees! I'm begging you, can't you see? Just do me this favour, I'll never forget it. Dearest friend, please, don't be so obstinate!

Podkolyosin I'm sorry, old chap, I honestly can't.

Kochkaryov (*rising, angrily*) Swine!

Podkolyosin Go ahead, shout all you want.

Kochkaryov Stupid creature! You're unbelievable, you are.

Podkolyosin Go on, shout your head off.

Kochkaryov Who d'you think I've done all this for? Who have I been knocking my brains out for? This is for your benefit, you idiot! I mean, what do I care, eh? I'm finished with you, that's it.

Podkolyosin Who asked you to get involved anyway? Just drop it, all right?

Kochkaryov Yes, and you'll be lost without me, you can't do anything without me. If I don't find you a wife you'll be an idiot the rest of your days!

Podkolyosin And what's that to you?

Kochkaryov Look, it's for your sake I'm making all this effort, you numskull.

Podkolyosin I don't want your efforts.

Kochkaryov Oh, go to hell, then!

Podkolyosin Right, I'll just do that!

Kochkaryov And *bon voyage*, sir!

Podkolyosin Yes, I'll go all right.

Kochkaryov Go on, go on, I hope you break your damn leg on the way! From the bottom of my heart, I hope some drunken cab-driver rams his shaft down your gullet! Huh, civil servant? You're a rag, sir! That's it, it's all over between us, I swear to God. And don't let me set eyes on you ever again!

Podkolyosin I won't! (*Exits.*)

Kochkaryov Go on, go to your old friend! Go to the devil, sir! (*Opening the door, shouts after him.*) Idiot! (*Paces up and down the room in great agitation.*) Dear God, has the world ever seen his like, eh? What an idiot! Actually, to tell the truth, I'm not much better. Come on, be my witness, I appeal to you – aren't I an idiot too? A prize ass? What am I beating my brains out for, shouting myself hoarse? I mean, what is he to me? A relative or what? And what am I to him? His auntie, his mother-in-law, his old nanny? What demon possessed me to get mixed up in his affairs, worrying myself sick? Damn the man, why did I do it? I haven't a clue. You might as well ask why people do anything! What a swine! What a repulsive, nasty clock he's got! You dumb animal, I'd like to smack you right on the nose, the ears, the mouth, the teeth – all over! (*Punches the air in fury.*) You know, what really annoys me is that he's cleared off – he doesn't give a damn. It's like water off a duck's back, that's what I can't stand. He'll go to his flat now, have a lie down and smoke his pipe, the disgusting creature! God knows, there are plenty of ugly mugs in the world, but he takes the biscuit. You couldn't imagine a worse, that's for sure. Well, what the hell, I'll just have to bring him back, the idle wretch. He's not sneaking away this time, I'll go and get the swine! (*Hurries out.*)

Agafya *enters.*

Agafya (*alone*) Honestly, my heart's beating so fast, I can't understand it. Everywhere I turn, it's as if I see

Mr Podkolyosin. You can't escape your fate, that's so true. I've been trying my utmost to think of other things, but no matter what I do ... I've tried winding wool, embroidering a purse – Mr Podkolyosin keeps coming into my mind. (*A pause.*) So, I'm finally about to take the plunge. They'll come and lead me into the church ... then they'll leave me alone with a man – ooh! I'm trembling all over. Farewell to my life as a single girl. (*Weeps.*) All these years I've lived in peace ... just getting on with my life, and now I'm to be married! The troubles that lie ahead of me! Children – little boys are such quarrelsome creatures, and there'll be little girls too. They'll grow up and have to be married. It's all very well if they find decent husbands, but what if they're drunkards, or the sort of men who'll gamble the shirt off their backs, on the turn of a card! (*Starts quietly sobbing again.*) I didn't have much fun when I was single, and I'm not even twenty-seven yet ... (*Changing her tone.*) But what on earth's keeping Mr Podkolyosin?

Enter **Podkolyosin**, *thrust on stage through the door by* **Kochkaryov** *at arm's length.*

Podkolyosin (*stammering*)   Ma'am, I've come to discuss one small point with you ... only I'd first like to know if you won't perhaps think it strange?

Agafya (*lowering her eyes*)   What is it?

Podkolyosin   No, ma'am, you must tell me first: you won't think it strange?

Agafya (*as before*)   Sir, I can't, till I know what it is.

Podkolyosin   But admit it, ma'am – you probably *will* think what I have to say is strange.

Agafya   Dear sir, how could I? I'll be happy to hear whatever you have to say.

Podkolyosin   Ah, but you haven't heard anything like this.

Agafya *lowers her eyes even further.* **Kochkaryov** *meanwhile enters stealthily and stands behind Podkolyosin.*

Podkolyosin   Anyway, the point is ... actually, perhaps I'd better tell you some other time.

Agafya   What on earth is it?

Podkolyosin   Well, I was meaning to tell you just now, but I keep having these doubts ...

Kochkaryov (*to himself, folding his arms*)   God Almighty, what a weed! He's not a man, he's an old woman's slipper, a mockery of a man, a satire on humanity!

Agafya   What doubts do you mean?

Podkolyosin   I don't know – just everything.

Kochkaryov (*aloud*)   Oh, this is stupid! Absolutely stupid! Look, ma'am – he's asking for your hand in marriage. He's trying to say that he can't live without you, he can't even exist. And all he wants to know is whether you'll consent to make him happy.

Podkolyosin (*almost panic-stricken, nudges him, speaking hurriedly aside*)   Good God, man, what are you doing?

Kochkaryov   So, what's it to be, dear lady? Do you consent to bring this poor mortal happiness?

Agafya   I wouldn't presume to think I could bring anyone happiness ... but yes, I consent.

Kochkaryov   Of course you do, of course you do! And about time. Now, give me your hands!

Podkolyosin   Just hold on.

He tries to whisper something in **Kochkaryov**'s *ear. He shakes his fist at him, glowering.* **Podkolyosin** *holds out his hand.*

Kochkaryov (*joining their hands*)   Well, now – God bless you! I give my consent and approval to this union. Marriage is a real business ... It's not like hailing a cab

and going off for a drive somewhere. It's a different sort
of commitment, a commitment which . . . Anyway, I
haven't time just now, I'll tell you about the
commitment later. Right, Ivan Kuzmich – kiss your
bride. You can do that now. You're supposed to do it
now. (**Agafya** *lowers her eyes.*) It's all right, dear lady, it's
got to be done. Let him kiss you.

Podkolyosin   With your permission, ma'am . . . (*Kisses
her and takes her hand.*) My, what a lovely little hand!
Where did you get such a lovely little hand, dear lady?
Now, if you don't mind, ma'am, I'd like the wedding to
take place within the hour.

Agafya   What, now? But isn't that perhaps rather
hasty?

Podkolyosin   No, not another word! I'd prefer it to
be even sooner, this very minute!

Kochkaryov   Bravo! Excellent! Good man! Yes, I must
confess I always expected great things from you! Now,
ma'am, you'd better hurry and get dressed. As a matter
of fact, I've already ordered the carriage and invited the
guests – they'll have gone straight to the church. And
you have your wedding dress ready, I know.

Agafya   Oh yes, it's been ready for ages. It'll only take
me a minute to put it on. (*Exits.*)

Podkolyosin   Thank you, thank you, dear friend! I see
everything you've done for me now. My own father
couldn't have done as much. And I can see that you've
acted out of genuine friendship. Thank you again, I'll
never forget your kindness. (*Moved.*) Next spring I'll
definitely visit your father's grave.

Kochkaryov   That's all right, old man – my pleasure.
Come on, I'll give you a kiss. (*Kisses him on one cheek, then
the other.*) God grant you a long and happy life . . . (*They
kiss again.*) contentment and prosperity . . . and a heap of
children . . .

Podkolyosin Thank you, dear friend. Now at last I realise what life is all about. A whole new world has opened up before me – I can see it all moving, pulsing with life, I can feel it sort of vaporising – I haven't a clue what's happening, but I've never seen anything like this before, I had no idea – I was simply ignorant, deprived of knowledge, I hadn't a serious thought in my head. I just lived from day to day like everybody else.

Kochkaryov I'm glad to hear it. Now, I'll go and check how they're laying the table. I'll be back in a minute. (*Aside.*) I'd better hide his hat, though, just in case. (*Picks up* **Podkolyosin**'s *hat and exits with it.*)

Podkolyosin (*alone*) I mean, really, what have I been up to now? Did I understand the meaning of life? I did not. I had no idea. And what sort of life had I as a bachelor, eh? What use was I? What did I do? I just went on living and working – walked to the office, had dinner, went to sleep. In fact, I've been the most ordinary, no-account man in the world. Only now do I see how stupid they are, those people who don't get married. And really, when you come to think of it – the sheer number of them, living in blindness! If I were a king somewhere, I'd order everybody to get married, absolutely everybody, I wouldn't have a single bachelor in my kingdom. It's a thought, though – in a few minutes, I'll be a married man. And suddenly I'll have a taste of that bliss you find only in fairy tales, something you can't begin to describe, there are just no words to describe it. (*After a brief pause.*) Still, say what you like, it *is* pretty frightening, when you think about it. Tying yourself down for life, for the rest of your days, come what may. And there's no getting out of it, no changing your mind, nothing – all wrapped up, done and dusted. And it's already too late to turn back – in another minute I'll be at the altar. I can't get away, it's impossible – the carriage is waiting, everything's ready, the guests are at the church. But is it really impossible?

Of course it is, absolutely. There are people at the door, they're all over the place. They'll want to know where I'm going. No, it's impossible. Hold on ... the window's open. How about the window? No, it wouldn't be right – besides which, it's too high. (*Goes up to the window.*) Hm ... it's not that high, just one storey, and fairly low at that ... No, how can I? I don't even have a hat. How can I go out without a hat? It's a bit awkward. Still, who's to say I can't go without a hat, what about giving it a try, eh? Shall we give it a shot? (*Stands up on the window-sill, and with a cry of 'God help me!' leaps out into the street. Moaning and groaning off-stage.*) Ouch! That *was* too high! Hey, cabby!

Cabman (*off-stage*)   Where to, sir?

Podkolyosin (*off-stage*)   Kanavka, near the Semyonov Bridge.

Cabman (*off-stage*)   Ten kopecks, take it or leave it.

Podkolyosin (*off-stage*)   Right! Let's go!

The rattle of the departing carriage is heard. **Agafya**, *now in her wedding dress, enters timidly, her head bowed.*

Agafya   Oh, I don't know what's the matter with me! I feel embarrassed again, and I'm trembling all over. Oh! I wish he weren't in the room, even for just a minute – if only he'd gone out for something! (*Looks round timidly.*) Where is he? There's no one here. Where can he have gone? (*Opens the door into the hall and calls.*) Fyokla, where has Mr Podkolyosin gone?

Fyokla (*off-stage*)   He's in there.

Agafya   What d'you mean, in there?

Fyokla (*entering*)   Why, he was sitting right here.

Agafya   But you can see for yourself, he isn't here.

Fyokla   Well, he certainly didn't come out – I was sitting in the hall.

Agafya So where is he, then?

Fyokla I've no idea. Maybe he went out by the back stairs, or maybe he's in Arina's room.

Agafya Auntie! Auntie!

Arina enters, all dressed up.

Arina What is it?

Agafya Is Mr Podkolyosin with you?

Arina No, he's supposed to be here. He hasn't been in to see me.

Fyokla And he definitely wasn't in the hall, I've been sitting there all the time.

Agafya Well, he's not here either, as you can see.

Kochkaryov enters.

Kochkaryov What's going on?

Agafya Mr Podkolyosin isn't here.

Kochkaryov Not here? What, has he left?

Agafya No, he hasn't left.

Kochkaryov What d'you mean? He's not here, but he hasn't left?

Fyokla I can't think where he can have got to. I was sitting in the hall the whole time, I never left my seat.

Arina Well, there's no way he could've gone down the back stairs.

Kochkaryov Dammit, he can't just have vanished without leaving the room! He must be hiding somewhere, surely? Podkolyosin! Where are you? Come on, stop playing the fool, that's enough. What kind of a joke is this? It's time you were in church! (*Looks behind the cupboard, even casts a sidelong glance under the chairs.*) This is incredible! He couldn't have left, he couldn't possibly!

He's here all right, his hat's in the other room, I put it there deliberately.

Arina   Why don't we ask the maid? She was outside the whole time, she might know something . . .
Dunyashka! Dunyashka!

Dunyashka *enters.*

Arina   Where's Mr Podkolyosin? Have you seen him?

Dunyashka   Yes, ma'am. The gentleman jumped out of the window.

Agafya *lets out a shriek, flings up her hands.*

All three   The window?

Dunyashka   Yes ma'am. Then he took a cab and drove off.

Arina   Are you telling the truth?

Kochkaryov   You're lying. It's not possible.

Dunyashka   I swear to God, sir, he did jump out. The man in the grocer's shop saw him too. He took a cab for ten kopecks and drove off.

Arina (*advancing on* **Kochkaryov**)   What's the meaning of this, sir, are you making fools of us? Having a good laugh at us? What have we done to deserve this, eh? This is shameful! In all my fifty-odd years I've never been so humiliated! By God, sir, you might be an honest man, but I'll spit in your face for this! Because even if you are an honest man, sir, this makes you a scoundrel, to shame a young girl like that in front of the whole world! I'm only a peasant woman, sir, but I wouldn't dream of doing such a thing, and you're supposed to be a gentleman! Well, you're obviously enough of a gentleman to play dirty tricks on people, and swindle them!

Makes a furious exit, taking **Agafya** *with her.* **Kochkaryov** *stands as if thunderstruck.*

Fyokla Well, well – so this is the person who can do the business! Knows how to fix up a match without a matchmaker! Well, I may have some queer fish on my books, all kinds of riff-raff, but I've got nobody that jumps out of windows, thank you very much!

Kochkaryov This is ridiculous! I don't believe it, I'll run and bring him back! (*Exits.*)

Fyokla Yes, do, bring him back! A fat lot you know about the marriage business! If he'd run out the door, it'd be a different story, but when a bridegroom jumps out of the window that's really something!

Curtain.

The Gamblers

Deeds of days long past

Characters

Ikharev
Gavryushka, *his manservant*
Aleksei, *a waiter*
Krugel
Shvokhnev
Uteshitelny
Glov, *Mikhail Aleksandrovich, an old man*
Young Glov, *Aleksandr Mikhailovich, his son*
Zamukhryshkin, *a bank clerk*

The scene is a room in a provincial tavern. **Ikharev** *enters, accompanied by the waiter* **Aleksei** *and his manservant* **Gavryushka**.

Aleksei Go right on in, sir, it's a nice little room! You'll have peace and quiet here, sir, no noise at all.

Ikharev Hm, no noise, maybe, but what about the cavalry, the little gallopers, eh?

Aleksei Does your honour mean fleas? No, you can set your mind at ease, sir. If a flea or bedbug bites you, sir, we accept full responsibility. We make a point of that.

Ikharev (*to* **Gavryushka**) Fetch my things in from the carriage.

Gavryushka *exits.*

Ikharev (*to* **Aleksei**) So, what's your name?

Aleksei Aleksei, sir.

Ikharev Right then, listen . . . (*Meaningfully.*) Tell me, who else is staying here?

Aleksei Oh, a lot of people now. Practically all the rooms are taken.

Ikharev Who exactly?

Aleksei Well, there's Mr Shvokhnev, Colonel Krugel, Mr Uteshitelny . . .

Ikharev Do they play cards?

Aleksei Sir, they've been playing cards for six nights on the trot.

Ikharev Right, here's a couple of roubles! (*Thrusts them into his hand.*)

Aleksei (*bowing*) Thank you very much, sir.

Ikharev And there'll be more to come.

Aleksei   Much obliged to you, sir.

Ikharev   So, do they play amongst themselves?

Aleksei   Oh no, sir, no, they cleaned out Lieutenant Artunovsky just the other day, and they took Prince Shenkin for thirty-six thousand.

Ikharev   Good, here's another ten roubles! And if you play straight with me, you'll get even more. Tell me this – did you buy the cards?

Aleksei   No, sir – they've been using their own.

Ikharev   Where do they get them?

Aleksei   From a shop in town, sir – Vakhrameikin's.

Ikharev   That's a lie, you scoundrel!

Aleksei   I swear to God, sir.

Ikharev   All right. You and I'll have a chat later.

Gavryushka *carries in a box.*

Ikharev   Put it down here. Now, go and get me some water, I need a wash and shave.

The servants exit. **Ikharev** *then opens up the box, which is crammed full of packs of cards.*

What a sight, eh? Every pack a little goldmine. Took some hard work, too, plenty of sweat. Yes, easier said than done. My eyes are still glazed from putting the damn marks on them. Well, what the hell, it's an investment. Sort of thing you can hand down to your children. Look at this one – a perfect treasure, a pearl beyond price! I've even given it a name, yes, I have: Adelaida. Now, you do me a good turn, sweetheart, the way your dear sister did – you win me another eighty thousand, and when I get back home, I'll put up a marble statue to you. I'll order one in Moscow.

Hearing a noise, he hurriedly closes the box. Enter **Aleksei** *and*

Gavryushka, *carrying a wash-basin and stand, and a towel.*

Ikharev So, where are these gentlemen now? Are they in?

Aleksei Yes, sir, they're in the saloon.

Ikharev Right, I'll have a look at them, see what they're like. (*Exits.*)

Aleksei So, have you come a long way?

Gavryushka From Ryazan.

Aleksei And is that where you're from?

Gavryushka No, we're from Smolensk.

Aleksei Really? So your master lives in Smolensk?

Gavryushka No, not in Smolensk. He's got a hundred serfs in Smolensk, and another eighty in Kaluga.

Aleksei I see, he's got property in two places, then?

Gavryushka That's right. In the house alone we've got Ignaty, the butler, Pavlushka, who used to travel round with my master, there's Gerasim the footman, Ivan, he's a footman too, there's Ivan the whipper-in, Ivan again, the fiddler, then there's Grigory the cook, Semyon the cook, Varukh the gardener, Dementy the coachman – and that's about the lot!

Krugel and **Shvokhnev** *enter warily.*

Krugel Listen, I'm worried – what if he finds us here?

Shvokhnev He won't – Uteshitelny'll keep him busy. (*To* **Aleksei**.) Off you go, lad, they're calling you!

Aleksei *exits.* **Shvokhnev** *quickly goes up to* **Gavryushka**.

Shvokhnev So, where's your master from?

Gavryushka Well, he's come from Ryazan just now.

Shvokhnev Is he a landowner?

Gavryushka He is, sir.

Shvokhnev Does he play cards?

Gavryushka He does, sir.

Shvokhnev Right, here's ten roubles for you. (*Gives him a banknote.*) Now, let's have the whole story!

Gavryushka You won't tell my master?

Both No, no, have no fear!

Shvokhnev How's he doing, is he on a winning streak, eh?

Gavryushka Well, do you know Colonel Chebotaryov?

Shvokhnev No, what about him?

Gavryushka We cleaned him out three weeks ago. Eighty thousand roubles, plus a fine Warsaw carriage, a box and a rug, and his gold epaulettes, no less – got six hundred roubles for them alone, once we'd melted them down.

Shvokhnev (*looks meaningfully at* **Krugel**) Eighty thousand, eh?

Krugel *shakes his head.*

Shvokhnev What, something fishy? Well, we'll find out in a minute. (*To* **Gavryushka**.) Listen, what does your master do when he's at home by himself?

Gavryushka What does he do? That's obvious, surely. He's a gentleman, sir, and he behaves like one – he doesn't do a thing.

Shvokhnev You're lying – I bet he's never without a card in his hand.

Gavryushka Well, I can't say, sir – I've only been

with him a fortnight. Used to be Pavlushka that
travelled with him. We've got Gerasim, the footman,
too, and Ivan, another footman, Ivan the whipper-in,
Ivan the fiddler, Dementy the coachman – and they
took on a new man from the village, just the other day.

Shvokhnev (*to* **Krugel**) What d'you reckon – a
cardsharp?

Krugel Very likely.

Shvokhnev Anyway, we'll try him out, it's worth a
shot.

They hurry out.

Gavryushka (*alone*) Well, they're quick off the mark.
Still, the money'll come in handy. This'll do for a
bonnet for Matryona, and sweets for the little rascals.
Oh, I do like the travelling life! You're always picking
up something or other: the master sends you out to buy
something, you can pocket a few coppers out of every
rouble. They've got some life, the gentry, when you
think about it. Just up and go wherever you like. He
gets fed up with Smolensk, so he clears off to Ryazan;
he doesn't fancy Ryazan, he goes on to Kazan. He
doesn't like Kazan, he takes himself off to Yaroslavl. I
still can't make my mind up which town's got more class
– Ryazan or Kazan? Kazan's actually classier, in Kazan
you can . . .

Ikharev *enters.*

Ikharev They're nothing special, as far I can see.
Even so . . . damn, I'd really love to take them to the
cleaners! Oh God, wouldn't I just! Even thinking about
it's making my heart thump. (*He takes out a shaving-brush
and soap, sits in front of the mirror, and begins to shave.*) Look,
my hand's shaking, I can hardly shave.

Aleksei (*enters*) Would you care for something to eat,
sir?

Ikharev   Yes, of course. Bring me lunch for four. Caviare, smoked salmon, four bottles of wine. Oh, and you can feed him too. (*Pointing to* **Gavryushka**.)

Aleksei (*to* **Gavryushka**)   Right, yours is in the kitchen, on you go.

Gavryushka *exits.*

Ikharev (*continues shaving*)   Now then – did they give you much?

Aleksei   Who, sir?

Ikharev   Come on, don't play the innocent – tell me!

Aleksei   Well, yes, sir – they did give me something for my pains.

Ikharev   How much? Fifty roubles?

Aleksei   Yes, sir. Fifty roubles.

Ikharev   Well, you won't get just fifty from me. Look, see that hundred-rouble note on the table? Take it. Go on, what are you afraid of? It won't bite. All I want out of you is honesty – you catch my drift? I don't care where the cards come from, Vakhrameikin or whoever, it's none of my business, but I'm making you a present of another dozen. (*Gives him a dozen packs of cards.*) D'you understand?

Aleksei   Of course I do. You can trust me, your honour, I know what I'm doing.

Ikharev   And keep the cards well out of sight, in case they search you.

Puts down his shaving-brush and soap, and wipes his face with the towel. **Aleksei** *exits.*

Ikharev   Mm, that'd be something – that'd be just dandy. Yes, I must admit – I'd really enjoy skinning that lot.

Shvokhnev, **Krugel** *and* **Uteshitelny** *all enter, bowing*.

Ikharev (*bows and goes to greet them*) Gentlemen, you must forgive me – this room isn't exactly luxurious. Four chairs, and that's about it.

Uteshitelny Sir, a warm welcome from one's host is worth more than any comfort.

Shvokhnev The room doesn't matter, it's the company that counts.

Uteshitelny That's very true. I couldn't exist without good company. (*To* **Krugel**.) You remember, dear sir, how I arrived here? On my own, a total stranger, didn't know a soul. Yes, and just picture it – the landlady's an old bat and there's a chambermaid on the stairs, ugly as sin. And I see some miserable army type hovering round her, drooling, he's obviously desperate ... I tell you, I was bored stiff. But all of a sudden Fate sent this gentleman, chance flung us together ... well, you've no idea how delighted I was! I simply can't last an hour without congenial company. I want to open my heart to everybody I meet.

Krugel That's a vice in you, my friend, not a virtue. Any sort of excess is bad. I'll bet you've been taken in a few times.

Uteshitelny Yes, certainly, I've been cheated, and I always will be. Even so, I can't help being open with people.

Krugel Well, I must say I find that incomprehensible – pouring your heart out to just anybody. Friends are a different matter.

Uteshitelny True, but man belongs to society.

Krugel Not all of him, though.

Uteshitelny Yes, all of him.

Krugel No, not all of him.

Uteshitelny Yes, all of him.

Krugel No, not all of him!

Uteshitelny Yes, all of him!

Shvokhnev (*to* **Uteshitelny**) Look, don't argue, sir, you're wrong.

Uteshitelny (*heatedly*) No, no, I can prove it. It's an obligation ... It's ... it's ... it's ... it's a moral duty! It's ... it's ... it's ...

Shvokhnev See, he's off again! He gets so worked up: you can make sense of the first couple of words, but after that it's anybody's guess.

Uteshitelny I can't help it! When it's an issue of principle, or duty, I lose my head completely. I usually warn people in advance: 'Gentlemen,' I say, 'if that sort of subject's going to come up, I'll get carried away, for sure.' It's a form of intoxication, my blood simply boils, and that's a fact.

Ikharev (*to himself*) Oh no, my friend. We all know the kind of people who get all hot and bothered at the mention of 'duty'. No doubt your blood is boiling, but not on that account. (*Aloud.*) Well then, gentlemen, while we're on the topic of sacred duty, why don't we sit down and have a little game of bank?

During the remainder of their conversation, lunch is set out on the table.

Uteshitelny Yes, why not, as long as the stakes aren't too high.

Krugel I'm not averse to harmless amusements.

Ikharev What about cards – d'you think they'll have some in this inn?

Shvokhnev Oh, you only have to ask.

Ikharev Cards, please!

Aleksei *prepares the card-table.*

Ikharev Meanwhile, gentlemen – be my guests!
(*Indicates the lunch table and goes over to it.*) The smoked
salmon's not up to much, I'm afraid, but the caviare's
pretty fair.

Shvokhnev (*popping a piece of salmon into his mouth*)
Actually, the salmon's fine.

Krugel And the cheese is excellent. Mm, the caviare's
not bad either.

Shvokhnev (*to* **Krugel**) D'you remember that
splendid cheese we had a couple of weeks ago?

Krugel I'll never forget the cheese I had once at
Aleksandrov's.

Uteshitelny Yes, but d'you know when cheese is at its
best, my dear sir? Eh? It's at its best when you have to
eat one dinner on top of another – that's when it takes
on its true meaning. It's like a good quartermaster then:
'Come on in, gentlemen,' it says, 'there's plenty of
room.'

Ikharev Well, come on in, gentlemen – the cards are
on the table.

Uteshitelny (*goes over to the card-table*) Ah, me – it's just
like old times! Look, Shvokhnev, see – the cards, eh?
How many years has it been?

Ikharev (*aside*) Spare me that!

Uteshitelny Perhaps you'd like to hold the bank, sir?

Ikharev Yes, why not? Not too much – say five
hundred roubles? Will you cut, sir? (*Deals the cards.*)

The game commences. Exclamations.

Shvokhnev Four, and an ace – I'll have ten on each.

Uteshitelny   Let's have that pack of yours, friend – I'll pick a card for luck, this is for the Marshal's wife.

Krugel   I'll add a nine, if you don't mind.

Uteshitelny   Shvokhnev, give me the chalk. I'll make a note of the stakes and keep score.

Shvokhnev   What the hell, let's double it!

Uteshitelny   I'll put in another five roubles!

Krugel   *Attendez*, gentlemen! Let's have a look at that – there should be two threes left in the pack.

Uteshitelny   (*leaps up from his seat. Aside*)   Damn, there's something fishy going on here. These are different cards, that's for sure.

The game continues.

Ikharev   (*to* **Krugel**)   May I ask, sir – are these both still in?

Krugel   Yes.

Ikharev   You don't fancy raising your stake?

Krugel   No.

Ikharev   (*to* **Shvokhnev**)   And what about you, sir? Are you in?

Shvokhnev   No, I'll sit this one out, if you don't mind. (*Gets up from his chair, rushes over to* **Uteshitelny** *and speaks in a hurried whisper.*) Damn the man, sir! He's switched the cards, he knows every trick going, he's a card-sharp of the first water!

Uteshitelny   (*anxiously*)   Yes, but we can't turn our backs on eighty thousand, can we?

Shvokhnev   We'll just have to, if we can't get our hands on it.

Uteshitelny Hm, that's a moot point, but meanwhile we'd better have it out with him.

Shvokhnev How?

Uteshitelny Come clean. Admit everything.

Shvokhnev What for?

Uteshitelny I'll tell you later. Come on.

They both go up to **Ikharev** *and clap him on the shoulder.*

Uteshitelny Well, sir, there's no point in firing off any more blanks!

Ikharev (*startled*) What d'you mean?

Uteshitelny And don't try and talk your way out of it. It takes one to know one, eh?

Ikharev (*politely*) Sir, if I might ask – in what sense am I to understand . . .

Uteshitelny Oh, absolutely straight – let's not waste words, sir, let's put our cards on the table. We've been observing your skills, and believe me, we recognise talent when we see it. On behalf of my comrades, sir, I propose an amicable alliance. With our know-how and capital combined, we can be vastly more successful than operating alone.

Ikharev And to what extent, sir, can I rely on the truth of your words?

Uteshitelny I'll tell you to what extent: we're prepared to come clean if you are. We'll freely admit that we'd planned to hang you out to dry, sir, but that was because we'd taken you for an amateur. However, now we see you're familiar with the higher mysteries. So, will you accept our friendship?

Ikharev After so cordial an invitation, how can I refuse?

Uteshitelny   Right, let's all shake on it.

Each in turn solemnly shakes **Ikharev***'s hand.*

Uteshitelny   Henceforth, we make common cause, and put aside all pretence and ceremony! May I ask how long you have been immersed in the secrets of our science?

Ikharev   Sir, it has been a passion of mine, I must confess, since my earliest youth. While I was still at school, I used to hold the bank for my schoolmates under the desk, during the teacher's lessons.

Uteshitelny   I thought as much. You don't acquire that sort of skill without long practice while you're still young and smart. Shvokhnev, d'you remember that extraordinary child?

Ikharev   What child?

Uteshitelny   Go on, you tell him.

Shvokhnev   I've never seen anything like it, it was quite unforgettable. His sister's husband (*Pointing to* **Uteshitelny**.) says to me: 'Shvokhnev, how would you like to see a miracle? An eleven-year old boy, Ivan Kubyshev's lad, can do card tricks better than any gambler. Drive over to Tetyushi and see for yourself.' Well, I set off for Tetyushi right away, I can tell you. I asked where Kubyshev's village was, went straight to his house, and got somebody to announce me. A worthy old gent came out. I introduced myself and said: 'Excuse me, sir, but I hear the Lord has blessed you with a most extraordinary child.' 'That's right,' he says (with none of these airs and graces, you know – that was something I liked about him). 'Yes,' he said, 'it's true, although a father shouldn't be singing the praises of his own son, but he certainly is a kind of prodigy. Misha,' he says, 'come out here and show the gentleman what you can do!' Well, then, a boy comes out, no more than a child, not even up to my shoulder, nothing special to look at.

Then he started dealing the cards, and I was just flabbergasted. It passed all description.

Ikharev   And couldn't you see how he did it?

Shvokhnev   Absolutely not, not a trace. And I had my eyes glued to him.

Ikharev   That's incredible.

Uteshitelny   The boy's a phenomenon!

Ikharev   You know, when you think about it – the sheer skill it takes, the sharp eyes, the careful study of the markings on the cards . . .

Uteshitelny   Ah well, that's considerably easier these days. Marked cards are old hat now. People try to memorise the key.

Ikharev   What, you mean the pattern?

Uteshitelny   That's right, the special design on the back of the card. In a certain town I know – which shall be nameless – there's a respectable gentleman who spends all his time doing just that. He gets several hundred packs of cards every year from Moscow – from whom, exactly, is shrouded in mystery – but his entire study consists of analysing the pattern on each card and working out the key. Look at this, he'll say, see how the pattern's set out on this two – and then how different it is on this other card! He can make five thousand a year easy, doing nothing else.

Ikharev   Well, it's no small matter.

Uteshitelny   That's how it's got to be done. It's what they call in economics 'the division of labour'. It's the same as a coachbuilder – I mean, he doesn't make the entire carriage himself, he farms part of it out to the blacksmith, and the upholsterer. It would take a whole lifetime otherwise.

Ikharev   D'you mind if I ask a question? How have

you managed so far to make sure your packs of cards get used? After all, you can't always bribe a servant.

Uteshitelny No, God forbid! It's too risky. You can give yourself away like that sometimes. No, we do things differently. This is what we did on one occasion: our agent arrived in town for the fair, passing himself off as a trader, and took a room at the local inn. He wasn't in time to rent a shop, so he kept his trunks and boxes in his room. Anyway, he stayed at the inn, ran up a huge bill, eating and drinking, then suddenly skipped town without paying. So the innkeeper searches his room, and sees there's nothing left but one box – he opens it up, and it's a hundred dozen packs of cards. Well, naturally, the cards are put up for sale right away at a public auction. They go for a rouble under the regular price, and the local shopkeepers instantly put them on show. And in four days' time the whole town's cleaned out!

Ikharev That's a neat trick.

Shvokhnev And what about the other chap, that landowner?

Ikharev What about him?

Uteshitelny Yes, that wasn't a bad piece of work either. I don't know if you know him – Arkady Andreevich Dergunov – he's a landowner, an extremely wealthy man. He's a first-rate cardplayer, scrupulously honest, there's no way you can put one over on him. He checks out everything himself, his servants are well-trained, real gentlemen, his house is a regular palace, his estate, his gardens, are all laid out in the English style . . . In brief, he's a Russian aristocrat in every sense of the word. Anyway, we'd been there three days already – how would we get the ball rolling? It seemed impossible, but at last we thought of a plan. One morning a cart comes flying through the yard, full of young fellows, blind drunk, singing and shouting, and driving hell for leather. Well, of course, the servants come running out to see the show, as they always do, gawping and guffawing, and they notice something's fallen off the back of the cart, so they run up and take a look – it's a suitcase. And they start waving and shouting: 'Stop! Stop!', but nobody hears them, they've already dashed off, you can't see them for dust. Anyway, they open the case and there's underwear, a few clothes, two hundred roubles in cash, and about forty dozen packs of cards. Well, naturally, they weren't going to turn down the money, and the cards went straight onto the master's table. And the very next evening, by the time the game folded, master and house-guests alike hadn't a kopeck left in their pockets.

Ikharev That's very clever. I mean, people might call that swindling and all sorts of names, but it's actually a subtle form of wit, the last word in refinement.

Uteshitelny These people don't understand gambling. There's no room for sentiment, the cards care for no man. Why, if my own father were to sit down at the table with me I'd skin him alive. Don't do it! We're all equal here.

Ikharev Yes, what they don't understand is that a gambler can be the most virtuous of men. I know one who can do anything with a pack of cards, yet he'd give his last kopeck to a beggar. Despite that, nothing on this earth would make him turn down the chance of teaming up in a threesome, to fleece some wretched mark. Anyway, gentlemen, since we're being so open, let me show you a wonderful trick. I take it you know what's meant by a composite, or selected pack – one I can guess any card from, at long range?

Uteshitelny Yes, I do – though it's maybe a different sort.

Ikharev Well, I think I can boast you won't find another one like this. It took me almost six months' work. Afterwards, I couldn't bear the sunlight for a whole two weeks. The doctor was afraid I had an inflammation of the eyes. (*Takes a pack of cards out of his box.*) There she is! And don't be annoyed, please, but she has a name, like a human being.

Uteshitelny   A name?

Ikharev   Yes, indeed. It's Adelaida.

Uteshitelny (*laughs*)   D'you hear that, Shvokhnev? Now there's a novel idea – calling a pack of cards Adelaida! Actually, that's quite witty.

Shvokhnev   Excellent! Alelaida! That's very good . . .

Uteshitelny   Adelaida – a *Fraülein*, no less. You hear that, Krugel? We've got a wife for you.

Krugel   What d'you mean? I'm not German. My grandfather was a German, but he couldn't speak the language either.

Uteshitelny (*examining the cards*)   This is a goldmine. There are absolutely no marks on it whatsoever. Can you really identify every card, from any distance?

Ikharev   Yes. I'll stand five paces away, if you like, and name every card you hold up. And I'll guarantee to hand over two thousand if I make a mistake.

Uteshitelny   Right then, what's this card?

Ikharev   A seven.

Uteshitelny   That's correct. What's this?

Ikharev   A jack.

Uteshitelny   Damn me, so it is. What's this?

Ikharev   A three.

Uteshitelny   That's incredible!

Krugel (*shrugging his shoulders*)   Absolutely amazing!

Shvokhnev   Absolutely!

Uteshitelny I'll have another look at this pack, if you don't mind. (*Examines the cards again.*) Yes, this is a wonderful object. She certainly deserves to have a name. I must say, though, it'd be hard to make proper use of it. Not unless with a very inexperienced player: I mean, you'd have to slip it in unnoticed.

Ikharev Well, of course, you can only do that in the heat of the moment, when the stakes are so high that even the most experienced players get agitated. But if you can distract a man just for a second, you can do what you like with him. It happens with all the best players, you know – they get 'played out', as they say. If a man's been at the cards two days and nights on the trot, with no sleep, he'll be played out. So in the heat of the moment, I can always manage to switch the cards. Take my word for it, the trick is to stay cool, while the other man's all excited. And there are thousands of ways of distracting somebody's attention. You can start a row with one of the other punters, for instance, tell him he's put down the wrong score. Everybody's eyes'll be on him, and meanwhile, the cards are switched.

Uteshitelny Well, sir, I can see that in addition to your skill, you also possess the gift of a cool head, and that's the main thing. Making your acquaintance is now even more important to us. Anyway, without further ado, let's drop all the formalities and regard each other as friends.

Ikharev Indeed, it's high time we did.

Uteshitelny Waiter, champagne! Let's drink to our amicable alliance!

Ikharev That's certainly worth drinking to.

Shvokhnev Yes, indeed – here we are poised to do great things, our weapons are in our hands, our forces are mustered – there's only one thing missing . . .

Ikharev Exactly, exactly – we need a fortress to

attack, and that's the trouble!

Uteshitelny What can we do? We've no enemy yet. (*Stares intently at* **Shvokhnev**.) What is it? You look as if you're going to say something, that we do have one.

Shvokhnev Yes, we do . . . (*Pauses.*)

Uteshitelny Ah! I know who you have in mind.

Ikharev (*excitedly*) Who? Tell me, who is it?

Uteshitelny Oh, he's talking nonsense. There's nothing in it. There's a country gentleman staying here, you see, name of Glov – Mikhail Aleksandrovich. But what's the point of discussing him, when he doesn't play cards? We've already had a go at him – I've been softening him up for a month. I've managed to gain his friendship, his confidence, even, but got simply nowhere.

Ikharev Listen, why not let me have a stab at him? It might work, you never know.

Uteshitelny You're wasting your time, I assure you.

Ikharev Well, there's no harm in trying.

Shvokhnev Yes, why not? Let's invite him in, anyway. And if we don't succeed, we'll just have a little chat. It's worth a try.

Uteshitelny All right, it's no skin off my nose. I'll bring him in.

Ikharev Bring him in now, by all means.

Uteshitelny All right, all right . . . (*Exits.*)

Ikharev Yes, you never know. Sometimes a thing seems quite impossible . . .

Shvokhnev That's what I say. I mean, it's not God you're dealing with, it's a human being. And a man's only a man, right? He'll say no today, no tomorrow, no the day after, but the fourth day – if you apply a bit of pressure – he'll cave in. Some of them put on an act, pretend they're unapproachable, but you take a closer look, you'll see there's no cause for alarm.

Krugel Well, this one's not like that.

Ikharev I hope to God he is! You wouldn't believe how desperate I am for some real action. I tell you, the last time I won anything was a month ago – eighty thousand roubles off that colonel, Chebotaryov. That's a whole month to get out of practice. You can't imagine how bored I've been. Absolutely bored rigid!

Shvokhnev I know the feeling. It's the way a general feels, when there's no war to fight. Yes, it's like the interval between acts, my friend, and it can be fatal. I know from experience, it's no joke.

Ikharev Honest to God, if somebody started to deal with five roubles in the pot, I'd pull up a chair.

Shvokhnev That's only natural. And that's how the most skilful gamblers come to grief at times. They're bored, they've no work, and out of sheer desperation they fling themselves at some miserable card-sharp, and get taken to the cleaners.

Ikharev So, is this Glov wealthy?

Krugel Oh, he's got money all right. Owns around a thousand serfs.

Ikharev God almighty! Listen, what about getting him drunk, send out for some champagne, eh?

Shvokhnev Never touches it.

Ikharev So what'll we do? How do we tackle him? No, hold on, wait a minute . . . you know, gambling's a huge temptation. I think if we could just get him to the table, he wouldn't hold out for long.

Shvokhnev Well, we'll give it a try. Krugel and I'll have a little game on the quiet here, very low stakes.

But don't take too much notice of him, these old types
are suspicious.

They sit off to the side with the cards. **Uteshitelny** *and*
Glov, *an elderly man, enter.*

Uteshitelny   Mr Ikharev, allow me to introduce Mr
Glov – Mikhail Aleksandrovich!

Ikharev   Sir, I've been so looking forward to this
honour. I mean, staying at the same inn . . .

Glov   And I'm delighted to meet you too, sir. It's just
a pity I'm on the point of leaving . . .

Ikharev (*pulling up a chair for him*)   Do sit down, sir,
please. Have you been in town long?

Uteshitelny, **Shvokhnev** *and* **Krugel** *whisper together.*

Glov   Oh, I'm absolutely sick of this town, my friend.
I'll be glad to see the back of it, and no mistake.

Ikharev   You're detained here on business, then?

Glov   Business, yes. A very troublesome matter.

Ikharev   A lawsuit, presumably?

Glov   No, thank God, not that, but a complicated
business just the same. I'm marrying off my daughter,
sir, a girl of eighteen. Perhaps you can understand a
father's position? I've come here to make various
purchases, but the main thing is to mortgage my estate.
The business ought to be finished by now, but the bank
still hasn't issued the money order.

Ikharev   And may one enquire, sir, how much you're
mortgaging your estate for?

Glov   Two hundred thousand. It should be cleared any
day now, but they're dragging their feet. I'm sick of
hanging around here. There are things to be done at
home, you know, and this doesn't leave much time. My
daughter's engaged . . . this is holding everything up.

I've already decided not to bother waiting.

Ikharev What? You're not going to wait for the money?

Glov Well, what can I do, sir? I mean, consider my position. I haven't seen my wife and children for a full month. And I don't receive any letters, God knows what's happening back home. I'm going to hand the whole business over to my son, he can stay here. I'm absolutely sick of it. (*Turning to* **Shvokhnev** *and* **Krugel**.) I'm sorry, gentlemen – I think I've disturbed you. You were busy with something?

Krugel No, nothing, really. We just started playing cards, to pass the time.

Glov But you have a bank there, I think.

Krugel Oh, hardly! A few coppers, for the fun of it.

Glov Gentlemen, gentlemen, listen to an old man. Of course there's no harm in it, just for amusement, and you're not likely to lose much playing for coppers, that's true, but even so . . . Oh, sirs, I've played cards myself, so I speak from experience. Everything in this life starts out small, but you wait and see – a small stake soon winds up a big one.

Shvokhnev (*aside to* **Ikharev**) The old fool's off on his hobby-horse now. (*To* **Glov**.) Now there you go, you see – making a mountain out of a molehill. That's always the way with old people.

Glov What do you mean? I'm not that old. And I'm going by experience.

Shvokhnev I don't mean you personally. But it is generally the case with old people. I mean, if they burn their fingers on something, they're convinced everybody else'll do exactly the same. If they're walking along the road, just gawping, and they happen to slip on the ice, they'll start shouting and pass a law that nobody's

allowed to walk on that road, because there's an icy
pach, and everyone's sure to crack their skull on it,
without taking into account the fact that other people
maybe don't gawp, and don't have slippery soles on
their boots. No, they don't take that into account. Some
man gets bitten by a dog – that means all dogs bite, so
nobody's allowed onto the street.

Glov   That's true, sir. That's a failing, it certainly is.
But you just look at young people – they're far too
reckless, they'll break their necks, and that's a fact!

Shvokhnev   Well, that's because there's no happy
medium – young people run mad, nobody can stand
them, but when they get old, they play the hypocrite,
and you still can't abide them.

Glov   You have a very low opinion of old people, sir.

Shvokhnev   What d'you mean, low opinion? It's the
truth, that's all.

Ikharev   Sir, if I may observe – you're being rather
harsh on . . .

Uteshitelny   As far as cards are concerned, I'm in
complete agreement with Mr Glov. I myself used to
play, gambled quite heavily. But, I thank Providence, I
managed to give it up. Not because I was losing, or
battling against fate; these things don't matter, believe
me. No, losing money is as nothing compared with
losing one's peace of mind. And the excitement of
gambling – I don't care what anyone says – it obviously
shortens your life.

Glov   You're absolutely right, sir – yes, that's a very
wise observation. However, if I may be permitted to ask
an indiscreet question: I've had the honour of your
acquaintance for some time now, but so far I haven't . . .

Uteshitelny   What is your question?

Glov   Well, sir, at the risk of seeming indelicate, how old are you?

Uteshitelny Thirty-nine.

Glov Good heavens! Thirty-nine, indeed! Why, you're still a young man. If only we had a few more people in Russia who could judge so wisely. Ye gods, what would it be like, eh? An absolute Golden Age. I thank my lucky stars I've made your acquaintance, sir, I truly do.

Ikharev And I share that opinion, sir, believe me. I wouldn't allow young people to touch cards, even. But why shouldn't responsible adults, people of mature judgement, be allowed a little harmless amusement? An elderly person, for instance, who can't dance?

Glov That's perfectly true, sir, but believe me, there are so many pleasures, so many duties – sacred duties, one might say – in our lives. Oh, sirs, take heed of an old man! There is no better calling for a man than family life, within his own domestic circle. All this you see around you, gentleman, is nothing but vexation of spirit, as God be my judge, and you have yet to taste true bliss. Why, I can scarcely wait for the moment I'll see my dear ones again, believe me. I can just imagine how my daughter will fling herself round my neck: 'Dearest, darling papa!' she'll say. And my son'll be home again from school, it's six months since I've seen him ... I can't find words to describe it, sirs, I swear to God. Well, after that, you don't even want to look at cards.

Ikharev But why should these feelings interfere with cards? Paternal feelings are one thing, cards are another ...

Enter **Aleksei**.

Aleksei (*to* **Glov**) Your servant's asking about the trunks. Do you want them taken out? The horses are ready.

Glov I'm just coming. Excuse me, gentlemen, I must leave you for a moment. (*Exits.*)

Ikharev Well, there's no hope there!

Uteshitelny I told you so. I don't know why you can't see it. I mean, you've only got to look at a man to tell if he's in the mood to play or not.

Ikharev Well, we should've had a proper go at him just the same. Why on earth did you back him up?

Uteshitelny There's no other way, friend. You've got to be very subtle with that sort, or they'll be onto you right away, they'll guess you're out to fleece them.

Ikharev Yes, but what's the result? He's clearing off now anyway.

Uteshitelny Just hang on, it's not over yet.

Glov *re-enters.*

Glov I'm most grateful, sirs, for the pleasure of your acquaintance. I'm only sorry we didn't meet earlier, but God willing, no doubt we'll bump into each other again.

Shvokhnev Oh, very likely. It's a small world, our paths'll cross for sure. If it's in the stars.

Glov Yes, indeed, that's perfectly true. If it's our fate, we'll meet again tomorrow, and that's the truth. Goodbye, gentlemen! My sincere thanks. (*To* **Uteshitelny**.) And I'm much obliged to you, sir, for relieving my solitude.

Uteshitelny Think nothing of it. It was my pleasure.

Glov Well, since you're so kind, perhaps I might ask for one more favour?

Uteshitelny What is it? Tell me. I'll do whatever I can.

Glov Put an old man's mind at ease!

Uteshitelny In what way?

Glov I'm leaving my boy Sasha here. He's a splendid young chap, with a good heart, but he's still rather immature – well, twenty-two, what would you expect? Barely a child. He's finished his studies, and all he wants to hear about is the cavalry. I keep telling him: 'It's too early, Sasha, wait a while, have a look round first. What do you want with the cavalry? Who knows, you might be more suited to the civil service. You've seen practically nothing of the world yet, and you've plenty of time!' Well, you know what young people are like. He's simply dazzled by the cavalry, all that gold braid, the gorgeous uniform . . . what should I do? You can't restrain their inclinations, can you. So, if you'd be so kind, my dear sir, and do me this favour . . . he'll be on his own now, and I've entrusted him with a few business matters. He's a young man, anything can happen, and I don't want the bank clerks cheating him – I mean, you never know. Anyway, I'd like you to take him under your wing, keep an eye on him, make sure he comes to no harm – if you'd be so kind, sir? (*Takes* **Uteshitelny**'*s hands.*)

Uteshitelny Why, certainly, certainly! I'll be like a second father to the boy, I'll do whatever I can.

Glov My dear sir! (*They embrace and kiss.*) You can always tell when a man has a good heart, yes, indeed! God will reward you for this, sir. Goodbye, gentlemen, and good luck – I sincerely hope you enjoy your stay.

Ikharev Goodbye, sir – *bon voyage!*

Shvokhnev I hope all's well at home.

Glov Thank you, gentlemen!

Uteshitelny I'll see you out, and help you into your carriage.

Glov Oh, sir, you're too kind!

They exit.

Ikharev   So, the bird has flown.

Shvokhnev   And he'd have been worth plucking!

Ikharev   I must confess, when he mentioned two hundred thousand, my heart leapt.

Krugel   My mouth's watering, even just thinking about it.

Ikharev   Yes, and when you think how much money just goes to waste, no use to anybody. I mean, what's the point of him having two hundred thousand? It'll all go on rags and frippery!

Shvokhnev   Yes, absolute trash!

Ikharev   And just think how much money never even gets into circulation! How much dead capital there is, like actual corpses, stretched out on bankers' slabs! Honestly, it'd make you weep. I'd get by quite happily with what's lying unspent at the Board of Trustees.

Shvokhnev   I'd settle for half of that.

Krugel   A quarter'd do me.

Shvokhnev   Oh, come off it, you're a German – you'd want more.

Krugel   I swear to God . . .

Shvokhnev   You'd grab our share.

Uteshitelny *rushes in, beaming delightedly.*

Uteshitelny   Gentlemen, gentlemen, our troubles are over! He's cleared off, and good riddance to him! The son's left behind. The old fool's authorised him to withdraw money from the bank and guess who's supposed to supervise him! He's a spirited lad, mad keen on the cavalry. Just ripe for the picking! I'll go and fetch him right now! (*Hurries out.*)

Ikharev Well done, sir.

Shvokhnev Bravo! Things are looking up!

They rub their hands in glee.

Ikharev Hooray for Uteshitelny! Now I understand why he was playing up to the old man. And all done so cleverly – so subtle!

Shvokhnev Oh yes, he has a real genius for that sort of thing.

Krugel An incredible talent!

Ikharev I must admit, when the old man said he was leaving his son here, the idea did flash through my mind, but only for a second, whereas he was onto it instantly . . . sharp as a tack!

Shvokhnev Ho, you've seen nothing yet.

Uteshitelny *enters along with* **Young Glov**.

Uteshitelny Gentlemen, allow me to introduce Aleksandr Mikhailych Glov, a first-rate young man and boon companion – take him to your bosoms, sirs!

Shvokhnev Delighted. (*Shakes his hand.*)

Ikharev Pleased to meet you . . .

Krugel We welcome you with open arms, sir.

Young Glov Gentlemen, I . . .

Uteshitelny Please, please – don't stand on ceremony. Equality, first and foremost, gentlemen! You can see we're all friends here, so to hell with etiquette!

Shvokhnev Absolutely!

Young Glov Right, then! (*Shakes hands with them all.*)

Uteshitelny Bravo, that's the spirit! Waiter – champagne! Now, sirs, have you noticed? Isn't there a whiff of the cavalry about him already? No offence, sir,

but your father ... well, we can speak bluntly, eh? He's
a bit of an ass, if you'll forgive my saying. I mean,
what's he thinking of, trying to turn this bold lad into a
penpusher? Anyway, young sir, is your sister's wedding
going to be soon?

Young Glov   To hell with her and her wedding! It
makes me so angry – it's because of her my father's
kept me stuck in the country for three months.

Uteshitelny   Tell me, is she quite pretty, your sister?

Young Glov   She's that all right. If she weren't my
sister I'd be after her myself.

Uteshitelny   Bravo, sir, bravo! Spoken like a true
cavalryman! Tell me, would you give me a hand if I
fancied abducting her?

Young Glov   Why not? Sure, I'd give you a hand.

Uteshitelny   Bravo, my lad! Dammit, that's what
you call a cavalryman, the genuine article! Waiter,
champagne! You're a man after my own heart, young
sir – yes, I do like people that speak their minds. Here,
let me give you a hug!

Shvokhnev   And I'll give him a hug!

Ikharev   And me!

Krugel   Well, if that's the way of it, I'll give him a
hug too!

Aleksei *brings in a bottle, with his finger over the cork, which
goes off with a pop and flies ceiling-wards; he fills their glasses.*

Uteshitelny   Gentlemen, a toast! Here's to our future
cavalry lieutenant! May he be first in battle, first with
the ladies, first to the bottle – in a word, may he be
whatever he damn well pleases!

All   Whatever he damn well pleases! (*They drink.*)

Young Glov   And here's to the cavalry! (*Raises his
glass.*)

All To the cavalry! (*They drink.*)

Uteshitelny Gentlemen! It's time we initiated our young friend into all the traditions of the cavalry! He can take a drink, that's obvious, but that's a mere bagatelle. He needs to be a do-or-die gambler! Do you play bank, sir?

Young Glov I'd love to – I'm desperate for a game, but I've no money.

Uteshitelny What nonsense! No money? All you need is your stake, and you'll have plenty of money – you'll win it!

Young Glov Yes, but I don't even have enough to sit in.

Uteshitelny We'll trust you for it, don't worry. I mean, you've got a bank draft, haven't you? We're happy to wait, and as soon they pay you, you can pay us – simple! In the meantime, you can give us an IOU. Ye gods, what am I talking about? As if you're a certainty to lose! Why, you might just as easily win several thousand in hard cash!

Young Glov But what if I do lose?

Uteshitelny For shame, sir! What sort of cavalryman are you? It's one of two things, naturally – you either win or you lose. But that's the whole point, that's the beauty of it – the risk. If there was no risk, anybody could do it. If there was no risk, penpushers would be heroes, and Jews would scale fortresses!

Young Glov (*with a wave of the hand*) Right, the hell with it, I'll play! Why should I mind my father?

Uteshitelny Bravo, Lieutenant! Waiter – the cards! (*Pours him a glass of champagne.*) Yes, that's what a man needs in his life – courage, attack, energy, that's what

counts ... Right, gentlemen, I'll hold the bank, at
twenty-five thousand. (*Deals to left and right.*) Now,
Lieutenant ... Shvokhnev, what are you betting? (*Deals.*)
What a strange sequence of cards. A mathematical
curiosity, no less! The jack's beaten and the nine takes.
What have you got there? And the four takes, too! Oh,
Lieutenant, you're a cavalryman all right! Did you
notice, Ikharev, the way he raised the stakes? An
absolute master! And the ace isn't even out yet! Come
on, Shvokhnev, fill the Lieutenant's glass! Aha! There
she is, there's the ace! And Krugel's scooped the lot!
Dammit, those Germans have all the luck! The four
takes, the three takes. Bravo, bravo, Lieutenant! You see
that, Shvokhnev? The Lieutenant's won nearly five
thousand already.

Young Glov (*bends a card*) What the hell, I'll double it!
Let the nine ride too, for another five hundred roubles!

Uteshitelny (*continues dealing*) Ho-ho! Go to it,
Lieutenant! The seven ... oh, no, he's folded, dammit,
the Lieutenant's lost! Oh well, my friend, it can't be
helped – you can't win 'em all, eh? Oh, come on,
Krugel, never mind calculating – put your money on the
card you've drawn! Bravo, the Lieutenant's up again!
Well, why don't you congratulate the man?

They all drink, and congratulate him, clinking their glasses.

They say the Queen of Spades always lets you down,
but I don't agree. You remember that little brunette of
yours, Shvokhnev? The one you used to call the Queen
of Spades? Where's she now, the little darling, eh? Gone
to the dogs, I'll bet. That's your card beaten, Krugel!
(*To* **Ikharev**.) And yours! Yours too, Shvokhnev – and
the Lieutenant's crashed as well!

Young Glov Dammit, I'll cover the bank!

Uteshitelny Bravo, Lieutenant! That's the true cavalry
spirit at last. Have you noticed, Shvokhnev, how a

man's true character will always emerge? Up till now, it
was clear that this young man would make a cavalry
officer, yes. But now – well, he obviously *is* one already!
Yes, a man's true nature . . . Oh, the Lieutenant's lost.

Young Glov Double it!

Uteshitelny Phew! Bravo, Lieutenant! The whole fifty
thousand? Now, that's what I call magnanimous, sir.
You won't find many people with that sort of character
– that's a heroic act, it is indeed . . . oops, the
Lieutenant's crashed again!

Young Glov Double it! Double it again, what the
hell!

Uteshitelny Oho, Lieutenant! A hundred thousand?
What a man, eh? And look at his eyes – look,
Shvokhnev, you see his eyes? Positively glowing! A
second Napoleon, it's obvious. Now, that's real heroism!
And the king's not appeared yet. Right, Shvokhnev, the
Queen of Diamonds for you. And a seven for you,
German – chew on that! Trash, nothing but trash. A
face card, that's all. I don't think there's a king in this
pack. Most peculiar. Ah, there he is, there's the king . . .
The Lieutenant's down again!

Young Glov (*excitedly*) Double it! Double it again,
dammit!

Uteshitelny No, hold on, my friend – that's two
hundred thousand you've lost already. You've got to pay
out first, otherwise you can't start a new hand. We can't
trust you for that kind of money.

Young Glov But where am I going to get it? I don't
have any money right now.

Uteshitelny Give us an IOU, then, and sign it.

Young Glov All right, I'll do it. (*Takes a pen.*)

Uteshitelny And hand over your bank draft too.

Young Glov   Here you are.

Uteshitelny   Now, just sign here, and here . . . (*Gives him papers to sign.*)

Young Glov   Certainly – I'll do whatever you say. Right, there you are, I've signed. Now let's play . . .

Uteshitelny   Hold on, hold on – let's see the colour of your money first!

Young Glov   Eh? Look, I'll pay you back, you can trust me.

Uteshitelny   No no, my friend, cash on the table.

Young Glov   What d'you mean? This is a vile trick.

Krugel   No, it isn't.

Ikharev   It's a completely different state of affairs. We're not on an equal footing.

Shvokhnev   Besides which, you might try and cheat us. It's a well-known fact, when somebody sits in with no money, they go all out to cheat.

Young Glov   All right, what do you want? Fix whatever you like, I'm game for anything – I'll even pay double.

Uteshitelny   Look, friend, what do we want with your interest? We'll pay *you* interest, as much as you like, if you'll lend us the cash.

Young Glov   (*in despair, decisively*)   Is that your final word? You won't play?

Shvokhnev   Bring us the money, and we'll start right away.

Young Glov   (*takes a pistol out of his pocket*)   Very well, gentlemen – goodbye! You'll never see me alive again! (*Runs out, with his pistol.*)

Uteshitelny   (*alarmed*)   Glov! Glov! What are you

doing? He's gone mad! I'd better run after him, in case he shoots himself! (*Runs out.*)

Ikharev   There'll be some scandal, if that maniac really does it.

Shvokhnev   The hell with him! Let him shoot himself if he wants, only not now – we haven't got our hands on his money yet. That's the annoying thing.

Krugel   You know, I'm scared. It's quite possible he'll . . .

Uteshitelny *returns, holding* **Young Glov** *by the hand, still gripping the pistol.*

Uteshitelny   Good God, sir, have you taken leave of your senses? D'you hear this, gentlemen? He was actually on the point of sticking the pistol in his mouth! For shame, sir!

All (*pressing round him*)   What are you doing? What's the matter with you?

Shvokhnev   An intelligent man, too – to think of shooting himself over a trifle.

Ikharev   I mean, at that rate, the whole of Russia should shoot itself: everybody's either lost at cards, or is going to. Otherwise, how could anybody win, eh? You can see that, surely.

Uteshitelny   You're an absolute idiot, if you'll forgive my saying. You don't know how lucky you are. Don't you realise how much you've gained by losing?

Young Glov (*irritated*)   What sort of fool do you take me for, eh? Where's the gain in losing two hundred thousand? Answer me that, dammit!

Uteshitelny   Honestly, you're a simpleton. Don't you see what glory awaits you in the regiment because of this? I'm not joking. What, before you're even commissioned you've lost two hundred thousand roubles?

You'll be a hero, they'll carry you around on their shoulders!

Young Glov (*cheered up a little*)   Huh, d'you think I haven't the guts to laugh all this off? If it comes to the bit? Well, to hell with it, and long live the cavalry!

Uteshitelny   Bravo! Long live the cavalry! Waiter, champagne!

The **Waiter** *brings in some bottles.*

Young Glov (*raising his glass*)   To the cavalry!

Ikharev   To the cavalry, God dammit!

Shvokhnev   Hooray for the cavalry!

Young Glov   What the hell, I don't give a damn! (*Sets his glass down on the table.*) The only problem is, how am I going to get home? My father ... oh God, my father! (*Clutches his head.*)

Uteshitelny   What do you want to go home for? There's no need.

Young Glov (*astonished*)   What d'you mean?

Uteshitelny   You can go straight to the regiment! We'll kit you out with the uniform and so on. Friend Shvokhnev, we'd better give him two hundred roubles now, let the Lieutenant have a bit of fun! He's got a girl already, I think I noticed – a dark-eyed beauty, eh?

Young Glov   Dammit, I'll go straight to her, take her by storm!

Uteshitelny   A regular cavalryman, eh? Shvokhnev, haven't you got a two-hundred rouble note?

Ikharev   What the hell, I'll give him it – let the Lieutenant have a right good time!

Young Glov (*takes the note and waves it aloft*)   Waiter, champagne!

All Yes, champagne!

*The **Waiter** brings in some bottles.*

Young Glov Long live the cavalry!

Uteshitelny The cavalry! You know, Shvokhnev, I've just had an idea . . . why don't we toss him up, the way they used to do in the regiment? Right, come on, grab hold of him!

They rush towards him, seize him by the arms and legs and toss him in the air, singing the familiar tune: 'For He's a Jolly Good Fellow!'

Young Glov (*raising his glass*) Hooray!

All Hooray!

They put him back down. **Young Glov** *smashes his glass on the floor, and the others do likewise, some on the floor, some under their boot-heels.*

Young Glov Right, I'm off to see her this minute!

Uteshitelny And we can't tag along, eh?

Young Glov Not a chance! And if anybody tries . . . it'll be sabres drawn!

Uteshitelny Hoho! A swashbuckler, eh? Full of passion and jealousy, an absolute demon! Gentlemen, I think this young man has the makings of a regular Don Juan, and fighting mad to boot! Well, goodbye, Lieutenant, we won't detain you!

Young Glov Goodbye!

Shvokhnev Come back and tell us how you got on.

Young Glov exits.

Uteshitelny We'd better sweet-talk him for a while, till we've got our hands on the money. Then he can go to hell!

Shvokhnev I'm only afraid the bank might drag its heels, paying out on his draft.

Uteshitelny Yes, that'd be rotten. Still, there are ways of speeding things up, as you know. No matter what, you've got to grease the odd palm if you want to do business.

Zamukhryshkin, *a bank clerk, pokes his head round the door. He is dressed in a rather shabby frock-coat.*

Zamukhryshkin Excuse me, gentlemen – is there a Mr Glov here?

Shvokhnev No. He's just gone out. What do you want with him?

Zamukhryshkin It's a business matter, sir – regarding payment on a bank draft.

Uteshitelny And who are you, sir?

Zamukhryshkin I'm an official of the bank, sir.

Uteshitelny Well, do come in! Please, have a seat. My friends and I take a lively interest in this matter, especially since we've just concluded a most amicable deal with young Mr Glov. On account of which, you may understand that these self-same gentlemen ... (*Points to each of them in turn.*) are prepared to express their gratitude most sincerely. D'you take my meaning? The only thing is, we must get the bank draft cashed as soon as possible.

Zamukhryshkin Well, be that as it may, it can't be done in under two weeks.

Uteshitelny That's a frightfully long time. You're obviously forgetting about our sincere gratitude.

Zamukhryshkin That goes without saying. We take that for granted. How could I forget it? That's why we're saying two weeks – otherwise you'd be hanging on for three months. We won't even get the money at the bank for another ten days, we haven't a blessed kopeck at the moment. We had a hundred and fifty thousand last week, but we had to pay it all out again. There's three landowners who mortgaged their estates in February, and they're still waiting.

Uteshitelny Well, that may be so for other people, but surely for your friends ... Listen, we must get better acquainted – we're all friends here, aren't we? What's your name again? Fentefley Perpentich, isn't it?

Zamukhryshkin No, sir – Psoy Stakhich.

Uteshitelny Well, it's pretty close. Anyway, look here, my dear Psoy Stakhich ... think of us as old friends, right? So, how are things? How's business, how's life at the bank?

Zamukhryshkin At the bank? It's a job, nothing special.

Uteshitelny Ah yes, but there's more than one way to make money in a bank, eh? To put it bluntly, sir ... are you getting your share?

Zamukhryshkin Well, you know yourself – a person's got to make a living.

Uteshitelny So, tell us the truth – are they all at it? At the bank, I mean – are they all crooks?

Zamukhryshkin Well, really! You're making fun of me, obviously. Oh, sirs – I mean, these people who write articles in the papers are forever going on about us taking bribes, but when you get right down to it, our superiors take bribes too. And as for you gentlemen, well – you might call it by a slightly grander name, a donation or subvention or whatever, but when you boil it down it's the same thing. A bribe's a bribe. What's sauce for the goose, is sauce for the gander.

Uteshitelny Oh dear, our banker's taken offence, I can see that. That's what comes of casting aspersions on a man's honour.

Zamukhryshkin   Honour's a ticklish business, gentlemen, as you well know. But I'm not offended. I'm a man of the world.

Uteshitelny   Well, anyway, let's have a little friendly chat, eh? Tell me, my dear sir, how are things? How's life treating you, Psoy Stakhich? How are you getting on? You have a wife and children, I presume?

Zamukhryshkin   I do, praise be. God's been good to me. I've two boys at the local school, and two little 'uns at home. One of them's still in a smock, but the other's crawling.

Uteshitelny   And I daresay they all know how to use their little hands, eh? (*Gestures taking money.*)

Zamukhryshkin   Really, sirs, you must have your little joke. You see, there you go again.

Uteshitelny   Think nothing of it, Psoy Stakhich, a word spoken in jest, that's all. I mean, you're among friends, right? Waiter! A glass of champagne for our good friend here! And hurry up! We really must get to know each other better. We'll drop in for a visit some time, how about that?

Zamukhryshkin (*taking the glass of champagne*)   Please do, sirs! I'll tell you quite honestly – you'll get a better cup of tea at my house than you will at the Governor's.

Uteshitelny   A free gift from some tea-merchant, no doubt.

Zamukhryshkin   What else? Finest Ceylon, too.

Uteshitelny   But, my dear sir, you don't do business with shopkeepers, surely?

Zamukhryshkin (*drains his glass, then leans forward with his fists on his knees*)   Well, it's like this: the tea-merchant in this case had to pay out a small fortune, mostly through stupidity. A landowner by the name of Frakasov was mortgaging his estate, and the deal was done, he was just waiting for his money the next day. He was going into partnership with the tea-merchant on some sort of factory. Well, as you can appreciate, it's no skin off our nose whether the money's needed for a factory or whatever, or who he's going into partnership with. That's no concern of ours. However, this merchant very stupidly let the cat out of the bag that he was in partnership with Frakasov, and that he was expecting his money from him any minute. So, we promptly sent word to him, that if he coughed up two thousand roubles he could have his money on the spot – and if he didn't, he'd just have to wait! Meanwhile all sorts of equipment had already been delivered to the factory, boilers and whatnot, and the suppliers were demanding their cash. Anyway, the merchant could see he was on a hiding to nothing, so he gave us the two thousand, plus three pounds of tea apiece. You can call it a bribe, but it was his own silly fault. Somebody should've told him to keep his mouth shut.

Uteshitelny   Listen, friend – about this little business of ours . . . We'll give you a piece of it, and you can do whatever you need to do with your superiors. Only for God's sake, speed it up, right?

Zamukhryshkin   Well, we'll give it a try. (*Stands up.*) But I'll tell you frankly, sir – what you're asking's just not possible. I swear to God, there isn't a kopeck left in the bank. But we'll do our best.

Uteshitelny   So, who do we ask for?

Zamukhryshkin   Just ask for me – Psoy Stakhich. Anyway – goodbye, gentlemen! (*Makes for the door.*)

Shvokhnev   Psoy Stakhich! Sir! (*He looks round.*) Do your best!

Uteshitelny   As quick as you can, please! We're in a hurry.

Zamukhryshkin (*on his way out*)   I've told you. I'll do my best.

Uteshitelny   Damn! This'll take ages. (*Pounds his forehead.*) No, I'll run after him, maybe I can do something – I'm not giving up that money! Hell, I'll pay him three thousand out of my own pocket! (*Runs out.*)

Ikharev   It'd certainly be better to get it as soon as possible.

Shvokhnev   Damn right it would! I mean, we need that money.

Krugel   Oh God, if he could just find a way to get round him!

Ikharev   Are your affairs really in such . . .

Uteshitelny *re-enters, in despair.*

Uteshitelny   Damn! Damn! Damn! It can't be done in under four days! I feel like banging my head against a brick wall.

Ikharev   Why are you in such a rush? Can you really not wait four days?

Shvokhnev   That's the whole point, friend – this is absolutely crucial for us.

Uteshitelny   Wait, you say? Do you realise we're expected in Nizhny any minute? We haven't told you yet, but we received a message four days ago, to get down there as fast as possible, and take some money, no matter what. Some merchant's brought in a load of iron to sell, for six hundred thousand roubles. He'll be closing the deal on Tuesday, and he'll have the money in cash. And another one arrived yesterday, with half a million's worth of hemp.

Ikharev   Well, so what?

Uteshitelny   What d'you mean, so what? Listen, the old men are staying at home, and sending their sons instead.

Ikharev   Yes, but will the sons definitely play cards?

Uteshitelny   Ye gods, where've you been all your life? In China? Don't you know what their sons are like? How they've been raised? I mean, the way these merchants bring up their sons, they either know nothing, or just enough to behave like landed gentry – certainly not merchants. So, naturally, all they care about is hobnobbing with officers, and getting pie-eyed. As far as we're concerned, they're ripe for the picking. The idiots don't even realise that for every rouble they take off us, they end up paying back thousands. Yes, your average merchant has nothing on his mind but marrying off his daughter to some general, and wangling his son a job in the civil service. And that's our good fortune.

Ikharev   But are these deals absolutely sewn up?

Uteshitelny   Sewn up? Of course they are. Otherwise they wouldn't have let us know. The money's practically in our hands. So now every minute's precious.

Ikharev   Dammit to hell! What are we sitting here for? Come on, gentlemen, we agreed to work as a team!

Uteshitelny   Yes, and that's where we have the advantage. Listen, I've had an idea. There's no need for you to hurry off just yet. You've got some money, eighty thousand roubles. Let us have that, and you take Glov's IOU. You'll collect a hundred and fifty thousand for sure, that's almost double, and you'll be doing us a favour. We need that cash so badly, we'd be delighted to pay you three for one, even.

Ikharev   Well, all right – why not? To demonstrate the bonds of friendship . . . (*Goes over to his cash-box and takes out a wad of notes.*) Here you are – eighty thousand!

Uteshitelny And here's your IOU! I'll run and fetch Glov right away now – we'll have to bring him in, make it all legal. Krugel, take the money to my room – here's the key to my cash-box.

Krugel *exits.*

Uteshitelny Oh God, as long as we can get away from here by this evening! (*Exits.*)

Ikharev Of course, of course. You don't want to waste another minute here.

Shvokhnev And I'd advise you not to hang around either. As soon as you collect the money, come and join us. I mean, with two hundred thousand, you could do anything, absolutely corner the market . . . Oh, I've forgotten to tell Krugel something, it's very important. Wait a second, I'll be right back. (*Hurriedly exits.*)

Ikharev (*alone*) Well, there's a turn-up! This morning I had eighty thousand, and by tonight I'll have two hundred thousand. How about that, eh? That's a lifetime's work for most people, hard toil, unremitting effort, depriving yourself, ruining your health. And here in just a few hours, a few minutes, – I've made a fortune! I feel like a prince! Two hundred thousand – that's serious money! I mean, where'll you find two hundred thousand these days? What estate, what factory's going to make you that kind of money? I'd be a right one if I'd stayed in the country, yes, I can just imagine it, chasing round after peasants and village elders, for a measly three thousand a year. So a decent education isn't a waste, eh? All that ignorance you pick up in the country – you'd need to scrape it off with a knife! And what would I be doing with my time? Arguing with peasants and elders, when what I really need is civilised conversation, with educated people. Well, I'm a rich man now, I can do what I like. I can devote my time to improving my mind. If I fancy a trip to St Petersburg, then St Petersburg it is. I can go to the theatre, the Imperial Mint, I can stroll past the Palace, along the English Embankment, through the Summer Gardens ... I can go to Moscow, have dinner at Yar's ... I'll be able to dress in the latest fashion, I'll be the equal of anybody, I'll do all that's expected of a man of culture. And where's it all come from? What do I owe it all to? Why, to fraud, as it's commonly termed. What nonsense! That's not fraud, no way! It doesn't take two minutes to commit a fraud, but this takes practice, long hours of study. Well, even supposing it is fraud, it's absolutely essential – you can't do a thing without it. In a sense it's simply prudence. For instance, if I didn't know all the tricks, if I wasn't up to the mark myself, they'd have swindled me for sure. They were going to cheat me, of course, but when they saw it wasn't some simple soul they were dealing with, well, they were obliged to seek my assistance. Yes, brains are a great asset. You need to be smart in this world. I have a completely different outlook on life. Anybody can go through life like a fool, there's no trick to that, but to live craftily, artfully, to cheat people without being cheated yourself, well, that's a genuinely worthwhile aim.

Young Glov *rushes in.*

Young Glov   Where are they? I've just been to their room, and it's empty!

Ikharev   They were here a minute ago. They've only just stepped outside.

Young Glov   What, have they gone already? Did they take your money?

Ikharev   Yes, we made a deal, and I'm supposed to wait here for you.

Aleksei *enters.*

Aleksei (*to* **Young Glov**)   Your honour was asking about the gentlemen?

Young Glov   Yes.

Aleksei   Well, sir – they've left.

Young Glov   What d'you mean, left?

Aleksei   What I said, sir. They've had a coach and horses waiting outside for the past half-hour.

Young Glov (*wringing his hands*)   Oh my God, we've been had!

Ikharev   What are you raving about? I don't understand a word of this. Uteshitelny's due back any minute. I mean, you know you've to pay your entire debt to me now? It's been transferred.

Young Glov   What damn debt! You've to collect my debt? That's priceless. Don't you see what a fool they've made of you?

Ikharev   What nonsense is this? You're obviously still suffering from a hangover.

Young Glov   Friend, it looks like we both are. Wake up, for God's sake! Do you really think I'm Glov? If I'm Glov, you're the Emperor of China.

Ikharev (*anxiously*)   What are you talking about? Don't be ridiculous. What about your father, and . . . and . . .

Young Glov   The old man? In the first place, he's not anybody's father, and never likely to be, damn him! And in the second place, his name's not Glov either, but Krynitsyn, and he's one of their gang.

Ikharev   Listen, listen – tell me the truth, this is no joking matter!

Young Glov   Who's joking? I was involved with them myself, and they've swindled me too. They promised me three thousand for my pains.

Ikharev (*goes up to him, vehemently*)   This isn't funny, I'm warning you! What kind of fool d'you take me for?

What about the authorisation, the bank draft . . . and the clerk who was here from the bank just a minute ago, what's-his-name, Psoy Stakhich? D'you think I can't send for him right now?

Young Glov Well, for starters, he isn't a bank clerk, he's a retired army captain, and he's part of the same crew. What's more his name isn't Psoy Stakhich, it's Flor Semyonovich!

Ikharev (*in despair*) Then who are you? Who the hell are you, eh? Tell me!

Young Glov Who am I? I'm a man of honour, sir, forced to become a swindler against my will. They cleaned me out, stripped the very shirt off my back. What was I going to do, starve to death? I agreed to get involved for three thousand roubles, to come in with them and hoodwink you. I'm telling you this straight, sir, so you can see I've acted honourably.

Ikharev (*in a fury, seizes him by the collar*) You damned scoundrel!

Aleksei (*aside*) Well, well, they're coming to blows now. Time I wasn't here! (*Exits.*)

Ikharev (*dragging him*) Right, let's go!

Young Glov Go where?

Ikharev Where? (*In a frenzy.*) Where? To the police, dammit! You're going to the police!

Young Glov Now, hold on, you've no case against me.

Ikharev No case? What, robbing people blind, stealing money in broad daylight, like a common sneak-thief! I've no case? Using confidence tricks! Yes, well, you can tell me I've no case from your cosy cell in Siberia, friend! You just wait, they'll catch up with that whole thieving gang of yours! You'll find out what it means to abuse the trust of honest, good-hearted people. I'll have the law on you, by God I will! (*Drags him out*).

Young Glov   Oh sure, you could call in the law all right, if you hadn't broken the law yourself! You just think about it – you joined forces with them in order to swindle me, sir. And the packs of cards were your handiwork, it was you that marked them up. No, my friend, when you get right down to it, you've no grounds for complaint whatsoever!

Ikharev (*pounding his forehead in despair*)   Dammit to hell! He's right! (*Slumps helplessly onto a chair.* **Young Glov** *meanwhile runs out of the room.*) What a damned diabolical trick!

Young Glov (*peeping round the door*)   Cheer up! You're not down yet. You've still got your Adelaida! (*Vanishes.*)

Ikharev (*enraged*)   To hell with Adelaida! (*Snatches up the pack of cards and hurls them at the door. Queens and deuces fly everywhere.*) Scoundrels like that are a disgrace to humanity, it's shameful! I'm about ready to go mad! The way they all played their parts, so fiendishly clever – father, son, that bank clerk. And they've covered up their tracks, too. I can't even lodge a complaint! (*Leaps up from the chair and begins pacing the room in agitation.*) You try to be clever, you try to use your brains, and what's the point, eh? You work out methods, you refine them – dammit to hell, it's not worth all that energy and commitment, not worth the effort! Some swindler suddenly appears and takes you to the cleaners! Some villain, at one stroke, tears down an edifice you've spent years building up! (*Waving his arms in vexation.*) Dammit, what a deceitful country this is! You need to be as thick as a post to have any luck, a brainless clod, with a greasy pack of cards, playing whist for peanuts!

Curtain.